CHOOSING A SEX ETHIC

CHOOSING A SEX ETHIC

A JEWISH INQUIRY

Eugene B. Borowitz

Published by SCHOCKEN BOOKS for
B'nai B'rith Hillel Foundations, Inc.

This volume is a selection in the *Hillel Library* series. Sponsored by the B'nai B'rith Hillel Foundations, it offers significant books of Jewish interest to university students. Written by men of variant points of view, the books are selected with special regard to their value as educational and literary resources on the university level, in the hope that they will stimulate the further discussion and study of issues in the foreground of student concern.

Fifth Printing, 1974

Manufactured in the United States of America

TO
ARNOLD JACOB WOLF

CONTENTS

SOME NOTES OF SPECIAL INTEREST

The Question

1

ETHICS IN THE MODERN MODE

SEX IS a personal and private matter. Ethics is a public and abstract discipline. "Sex ethics" thus seems to be a contradiction in terms. Moreover, when a rabbi seeks to speak on this subject, is he not bound by the teachings of his tradition? How freely can he respond, without preconceived notions or values, to the predicament of the person who stands before him in doubt or need?

There is much truth in these questions, and the attempt to preserve the valid insights they contain has determined the shape of this book.

To take the last question first. In religious matters, I am a liberal, perhaps more attentive than many to what the Jewish tradition demands, yet insistent that law or concept must change whenever necessary. Intellectually, I have been influenced more by Martin Buber than by any other single thinker. What he has taught me about being a person in our world informs much of this book. Practically, I became concerned with the question of sex ethics because it arose in numerous discussions with young people and adults, and I felt I could not deal with the issues responsibly without substantial further thought and study.

My conclusions as to what people ought to do in their sexual activity do not form the critical part of this book. More important for the reader and me is the method we employ to reach such decisions. I believe it is no longer possible to deal with sex ethics in the old-fashioned manner of consulting a book for rules or principles to guide one's conduct. Contemporary ethical discussion is, or should be, based on the principle of *autonomy,* or recognition of the independent value of each man's conscience. No one has the right to tell someone else what is right and thus imply that he should not think about it for himself.

Ethical procedure requires one person to encourage another to make up his own mind in as informed, thoughtful, and sensitive a way as he can. Each person's ethical autonomy is to be respected and encouraged to seek mature and responsible expression.

What the reader will therefore find in this volume is not a set of rules or prescriptions governing sexual conduct but rather an attempt to clarify the fundamental issues involved in the question of sex ethics. For this purpose, the book is arranged in four steps. First, the central question under discussion is specified in this chapter and the next. Second, four standards of sexual behavior are distinguished as representative of various standards currently advocated or suggested. The real ethical task is to choose between them. However, in this context the issue of contraception must be raised as a necessary precondition or ethical necessity; and before moving to a detailed analysis of the four options, the Jewish experience must also be reviewed to set them in relief. Third, the options are confronted in their most persuasive form in an attempt to determine what notions and beliefs about sex, man, and society seem to motivate them. The values we can discover in this analysis may enable us to determine which sex ethic is right or most persuasive to us. Finally, I present a summary of my own findings in the hope that it may help the reader test and integrate his own point of view and reach a thoughtful, autonomous conclusion.

This goal of autonomy may be beyond the reach of some people. All of us are the product of our childhood emotions, particularly in sexual matters, and many of us are so conditioned by familial or social standards, that we are hardly free to choose a new pattern of behavior. Moreover, such freedom can be frightening. Some who manage to achieve even a glimmer of it are so troubled by the responsibility of having to make critical decisions on their own, that they quickly flee to some authority to make their decisions for them. Generally, we tend to give up old standards for new only when we have changed our social context or reference group. For this reason, college has become a natural setting for changing one's thinking about sex morality.

Severed from home and community ties, the student meets new and different kinds of people, often with widely differing ideas about right and wrong. This situation encourages change, as does much of our society, with its emphasis on being creative, experimental—finding and doing "your own thing."

Yet no group, whether parents or clergy, dormitory mates or social clique, should be the ultimate source of personal ethics. As long as we do not establish our own standards of conduct, we are not autonomous, ethically not fully mature. To be a person of conscience implies a basic trust in one's own considered yet quite private judgment. It takes great courage to be self-reliant. It takes even more to stand up for one's mature decisions against the pressure of what others think, especially when they are the majority. But ethical decisions can hardly be subject to majority vote. For this reason, statistics on sexual behavior, though valuable as indices of certain kinds of reality, are ultimately irrelevant to the search for a sex ethic.[1]

Research data assembled during the past few decades indicate that a large majority of males and approximately one of every two females have had intercourse before marriage. The percentage among college students may be somewhat lower.[2] Of those who have had intercourse, between half to two-thirds of the women and a sizeable number of the men restrict their practice to the person they later marry. Comparative statistics since the 1920's indicate that there has been relatively little change in the proportions of men or women involved.[3] The greatest change for males has occurred among college men, who today are more likely to find their partners on campus than off campus.[4] Furthermore, present research indicates that premarital intercourse does not seem to have any noticeable effect upon the ease or difficulty of establishing a happy marriage.[5]

Two conclusions may be drawn from these data. First, many women and almost all men no longer abide by the old ethical ideal postulating that intercourse should occur only in marriage. Second, there is no evidence that a sexual revolution with regard to the practice of intercourse has taken place since the 1920's.

It should be noted that neither of these observations can tell us anything about right or wrong. Statistical analysis may show us that a standard of conduct which is disregarded by many people has become untenable and ought to be changed. Conversely, we may come to the conclusion that it is not the standards that require change, but people. Yet the central issue in an ethical investigation is not the number of people who are involved or the change in their behavior that can be observed, but whether what happens is right or wrong. We reach the ethical dimension when we make a judgment about the data—when by our decision we turn the quantitative material into a qualitative statement.[6] Ethics is the discipline of thinking about and making value judgments about right and wrong.[7]

The fact that a special chapter deals with the Jewish attitudes on this issue is not meant to imply that I believe there is a separate Jewish ethic for sex or, indeed, for anything else.[8] Either an ethical position is valid for everyone in a similar situation, or it can hardly be said to be ethical. The Jewish data, however, have special relevance to our problem. Jews have long been commended for what seemed, even to their enemies, to be the dignity and nobility of their sexual practices. Moreover, the Jews went through substantial institutional evolution in pursuit of these values and in response to social change. By studying the record of their accommodation as well as their resistance to change over the centuries, one may discover how one social group actually responded to some of the options currently being advocated. The student of human culture may find this diverse human experience intrinsically interesting, while the believing Jew may find that it offers him continuing guidance and facilitates his ethical choice.

2

SPECIFYING THE PROBLEM

THE ETHICS OF sexual behavior might well treat of such matters as masturbation, homosexuality, or adultery. These are real problems in many lives and must concern all who care about others. Yet they are not the central issue in sexual ethics today. But sexual intercourse without marriage *is,* for despite considerable change in our sexual attitudes most people are not yet ready to accept freer intercourse. We may consider it healthy that dating is common, chaperones are rare, kissing is not limited to the engaged, and that women's dress is fashionably revealing, but we are troubled by the parallel suggestion that, since so many peripheral sexual activities have been liberalized, it is time for the standards permitting sexual intercourse to be changed as well. Such a suggestion quickly draws cherished values and strong emotions into the discussion, and serious doubt about, if not strong resistance to, change arises.

The new, unanticipated social setting of the issue endows it with an immediacy our forefathers could not have known. The old fears connected with unrestricted sexual intercourse have now been substantially removed. Technology has conquered the threat of unwanted pregnancy or venereal disease, and changing values have made the loss of virginity less damning. Our culture is permeated on many levels with a Freudian interest in sex and the permissiveness of pleasure.[9]

The struggle for the equality of women has also been an important factor. Men formerly enjoyed a double standard of sexual behavior, one that allowed and sometimes even encouraged them to have intercourse freely. Such was thought to be man's nature and thus his right. But if women are now acknowledged to be entitled to the same rights as men and if female sexuality and sexual needs are to be as fully recognized as man's, should not women also be permitted freer sexual activity? This would make it possible for two free and equal parties, out of mutual desire, to agree to have intercourse without marriage. And it would be an ethical action by virtue of this free consent. The equality of women demands the end of the double sexual standard, with the result not that man must be more chaste but that women may be more free.

Modern women are as directly concerned with the problem of sex ethics as are men. I have therefore consciously tried to address the female as well as the male reader of this book, since we certainly cannot permit a double standard of ethical concern.

One freedom concerning sexual intercourse which is already widely practiced is the right to discuss it. What is commonly accepted today, particularly in academic and intellectual circles, was hardly thinkable a few decades ago. Even those who personally reject a more liberal sexual ethics are often able to accept the fact that many decent, unmarried young people do have sexual intercourse. Thus, the rightness of such sexual relations is a living question urgently put to us by the pressures of social change, and this discussion will be limited to the ethics of intercourse without marriage.

Three qualifications will help make the question less likely to lose its ethical and human focus. Two categories of people cannot really be expected to meet the ethical standard of responsible decision. First, there are the immature. They have not yet gained sufficient grasp of themselves or of their relation to the world to bring to so major a choice an appropriate personal depth.[10] I would venture the generalization that few high school students have attained the personal maturity required to deal with this question in full ethical seriousness. This generalization says less about young people than it does about our society and its ideas of child-rearing, but it draws our attention to an emotional reality we must recognize. Accordingly, the terms of this analysis are set on the level of those who have sufficient emotional and intellectual ability to think and make decisions with reasonable adult wisdom.[11]

Like the immature person, the neurotic is not free enough to reach properly ethical decisions.[12] His difficulty is most dramatically observed in the sexually compulsive person. Almost every campus has a certain population of promiscuous males and females. Their sexual behavior cannot be maintained as ethical, whatever their arguments to the contrary. And this is so not simply because of their promiscuity but because their acts do not stem from a real choice. Such people are driven by inner needs over which they have little control. Consequently, the promiscuous male is often someone who unconsciously doubts his own masculinity and so is forced unceasingly to prove to himself that he is a man. The promiscuous female is similarly often compensating by continually demonstrating to herself how desirable she can be.[13] Unconscious drives, not free will, rule their lives. They do not need more ethical information, for they are not free enough to use what they already have. They may need psychiatric therapy to be liberated from their controlling fantasies. If the treatment succeeds, it may bring them to the point where they, and not their infantile imaginings, may determine their choices. As a result, they may be able to lead an ethical existence for the first time.

The matter does not end there. One of the things Freudian psychology has taught us is the extent to which sexual energy is linked to a person's childhood experiences. Maturity in other aspects of personality does not guarantee maturity in sexual reaction or desire. When we confront our sexuality, an otherwise well-hidden neurotic nature may emerge. As a result, if we find ourselves being tied in emotional knots as we grow into an adult sex life (whether they take the form of a powerful push toward great indulgence or an equal impulse for complete withdrawal), we are not ready to discuss the ethics of sex. First we must clear up our emotional confusion. One would think sophisticated people who display neurotic behavior would readily acknowledge their need for psychiatric guidance. Yet many, though quite willing to talk about very intimate aspects of their sexual behavior, go silent when it comes to talking about felt emotional problems. Worse, they are too ashamed or proud to seek help.

At the same time, they may consider themselves experts in detecting someone else's neurotic tendencies. Most of us are "normal neurotics" and seek compensation in our sex life for what is bothering us elsewhere. It may be loneliness, failure at studies, disgust with the world, rebellion against parents, any of which may engender a desire to forget everything in the absorption of making love. If that is what leads us to seek sexual gratification, the ethical course would be to admit we are escaping and not try to supply noble justifications for our behavior.

The third qualification to be raised here concerns those people who are mature but whose sexual decisions are influenced by the reasonable certainty that they will never marry. In their case the normal ethical question of sexual intercourse is changed because of its unusual context. Perhaps the person will never know the meaning of a sexual relationship if this nonmarital possibility is bypassed. To say "no" may mean to say "never." Should a whole life be spent without sexual experience because marriage is not possible? Or in a less extreme version, perhaps the person has known the fulfillment of marital sex relations but now, after the death or divorce of the partner, is not likely ever to marry again. Should the rest of his life be empty of the joys of sexual relationship because they cannot be part of marriage?

These are serious questions, but they are not the proper object of this study because they raise the special case where intercourse is only possible, so it seems, outside of marriage. They are not the questions the overwhelming majority of people, and particularly young adults, face. For most of them the possibility of intercourse without marriage is present along with the probability that they will later marry. It is in this sense that we are concerned with the ethics of premarital sexual intercourse.

The Options

3

FOUR ALTERNATIVE ETHICS

A PERSON asking about sex ethics these days has, it seems to me, four major standards of practice from which to choose. One might easily elaborate others, but on closer examination they seem to vary from these basic patterns in detail rather than in substance. I will term them the ethics of healthy orgasm, of mutual consent, of love, and of marriage.[14] They are arranged here in ascending order of the demands they require for legitimate intercourse. Hence, the order of these positions is, roughly speaking, cumulative, and by working forward from the rationale of the most permissive criterion, one need only add on the more stringent criteria demanded by the subsequent positions.

The ethics of healthy orgasm judges sexual activity in terms of individual needs, pleasures, and fulfillment. Our new knowledge of human sexuality has taught us, despite the furtiveness and guilt which is our legacy from previous generations, that sex is fundamentally important to existence. Nonetheless, even with our new sexual sophistication, we are still often surprised to discover how extensively sex permeates everything we do. The refusal to accept this primary sexual energy and the insistence on repressing or denying it can warp or derange a personality. Body and soul alike are damaged by an inner flight from sexuality. If we are truly concerned with health, particularly in the sense of full well-being, then we must be concerned with a new sexual understanding of man.

Some generalized Freudianism of this kind often serves as the theoretical basis for this first ethic. It might then go on to argue, in a step far beyond Freud, that adults need the continual experience of satisfying orgasm, which is the culminating expression of all man's sexual urges and desires.[15] This satisfaction can be healthy only when it is achieved in heterosexual intercourse. To substitute lesser sex acts like kissing or petting, much less such sublimations as athletics or cold showers, is to revert to the old sick attitude toward sex. Sexual frustration was and is the pervading curse of our civilization. People snarl at each other and walk around desperately unhappy much of the time not because of some mysterious human condition, but simply because our society does not encourage the healthy experience of regular sexual relations. If all adults were living lives of full genital sexual self-expression—and even most married people today are not because of the old social taboos—then society itself would know a peace and joy which to our present, frustrated vision seems messianic.

This argument can be extended in either of two ways. One is toward mysticism, seeing orgasm not merely as a climax to inner need but as an opening to insight and creativity. To be denied the right to orgasm as a part of our regular ongoing existence is to be denied access to the expression of our deepest, most human powers. Man has not yet begun to give the world what he is capable of because the fundamental human style is to withhold and subdue the self rather than freely express it. Man rises to the highest peak of human experience in the sex act. It lifts us far beyond ourselves and floods our being with a sense of worth and richness. It brings us a moment of self-transcendence and union with the whole of the universe. For one glorious moment we are alive, we know, we are. Therefore, an intelligent person should make the continual experience of satisfying orgasm as fundamental to his life style as proper food, rest, and exercise.

A far simpler position is the one which argues purely on the basis of pleasure.[16] Without becoming involved in theories of sexuality or human creativity, it posits that the single most enjoyable thing most people can do is to have sexual intercourse. People want and need more gratification. They should be allowed to have as much of it as possible, for the tone of most of our existence is dull, if not positively unpleasant. No one could call our present sexual standards conducive to delight. They are so oppressive, that to deviate from them one must either risk great guilt or make the effort of conscious rebellion. Either way we cannot enjoy the new sexual permissiveness as much as we ought. In order to do that, we need a new standard of sex ethics founded on the principle of maximizing pleasure.

One need not look far to find persons who stand at, or close to, this end of the ethical spectrum. Hugh Hefner, the publisher of *Playboy* magazine, has given it a broad exposure in the long series of articles in his magazine entitled "The Playboy Philosophy." [17] His argument consists largely in the repudiation of a repressive Judaeo-Christian tradition as formalized in Western culture. The circulation and acceptance of his magazine have substantially increased because it feeds the male fantasy that only male desire has rights. Albert Ellis is a psychologist who has written seriously on the scientific aspects of sex. In approaching questions of value, he has often used his knowledge and prestige to write somewhat sensational "scientific" justifications of the orgasm ethic, e.g., *Sex Without Guilt* and *Sex and the Single Male*. For Paul Goodman sexual freedom is a major ingredient of the social revolution that he wishes us all to abet and that the young most desperately require. A similar Reichian romanticism has been given powerful literary form by Norman Mailer, most notably in his novel *An American Dream*. Yet Mailer's position, for all its fascination with the orgasm, seems closer to the second type of sex ethics, that of mutual consent. Some of the other men mentioned above may hold similar positions, yet in their radical call for sexual liberty they either forget about or momentarily set aside the question of the rights of the other person involved in the intercourse.

This second option would pose no objections to anything said about sex thus far. It would, in fact, utilize all the arguments listed above, adding, however, as a necessary condition, the free consent of the partner. The new emphasis is on the interpersonal aspect of sexual intercourse. Two people, not one individual, are involved. A person has sexual relations only because another is with him. Hence, the rightness of the act can be judged only when it is seen from the standpoint of both participants. Only when each is freely committed to it, can it be called "ethical."

The opposite is true of much contemporary sexual activity. The unethical aspect is most obvious in prostitution, where the consent of the partner is obtained by payment. The prostitute is rarely interested in intercourse for itself. She gives her agreement because she needs or wants the money. Since she permits the most personal human experience for impersonal reasons, prostitution is a common symbol for the worst kind of exploitation and immorality.

The more genteel may prefer psychological or sociological payoffs. But the refusal to take money only changes the means of payment, not the relationship, which is still a form of prostitution. Thus, when a man will date a girl only if she will grant him sexual favors or if a girl measures out sexual pleasures according to the quality of the dates she gets or what she thinks is required to hold on to a man, the economics may be different, but the relationship is still unethical. A similar exploitation often goes on in marriage. Marriage vows surely do not mean that every act of sexual intercourse, regardless of circumstances, is now justified. When a husband demands certain sexual rights because he is the provider, when a wife bargains sexual accessibility for budgetary privileges, will is being coerced through the exploitation of need. The marriage certificate cannot validate such immorality.

The critical consideration, then, is human autonomy, the right to a free decision. To violate another person's autonomy is to do him wrong. Sex is unquestionably important. Human dignity is even more important. Anytime one person uses power, of whatever variety, to infringe upon the freedom of another person or coerce his decision, he is acting in an unethical manner. Hence, the second option for a contemporary sexual ethics would be the pursuit of healthy orgasm, but only where it involves mutual consent.

Standing nearer to the third position, the love ethics, are such philosophers of the contextual as Martin Buber, such social scientists as Ira Reiss and Lester Kirkendall, such theological advocates of a new morality as Joseph Fletcher. Here the insistence upon free consent is considered an important addition to the criterion, but it is criticized as insufficient. It does not provide a standard for giving or withholding assent. However, the love ethic does, for it wants to reserve a special place in human relationships for sexual intercourse. Each sexual gesture has an appropriate value in a relationship and conveys a certain meaning to the partners. Sexual intercourse should not become a casual thing but rather be reserved for special relationships.

The drive to more common sexual intercourse seems part of a basic movement in our society. Everything private becomes transformed into a public matter. Nothing may remain hidden. Everything becomes part of the public domain, to be pictured, recorded, written about, discussed. What was precious because it was intimate now becomes worthless because it is so ordinary. This is one of the most disquieting aspects of our civilization. To be a human being means to be an individual—different and unique despite the masses of people in this world. As more and more of what is different about each of us gets swallowed up in the ritual conformity of similar clothes, similar education, and the expectation of living similar lives, anything that will legitimately preserve our distinctiveness is valuable. Men need some privacy to discover themselves, some private relations where they may be just themselves, some highly private acts they can share with only those who know their inmost individual selves. We shall not long be human unless we fight not just for the right to love but for the right to enjoy some acts only in the context of love. This is the social justification for the love ethic.

The personal justification is more readily accepted. Love means far more than mutual consent to acts of mutual benefit. Love is love precisely because it is a sharing of self, a giving of all that one is, a receiving without asking. It is a continuing openness, on the most intimate, individual level of lover to beloved. Two persons share their hopes, their fears, their wounds, their triumphs, and are thereby enriched. Should they not share their sexuality with one another? Should they not embrace each other in a physical unity as real as the one they have known as persons? For them the act of intercourse is appropriate. Yet, as the most personal and potentially the most creative of all human acts, intercourse should be limited to those with whom one is personally on a most intimate level. The ultimate intersexual expression demands a context of ultimate interpersonal concern. This is not a question of reserving intercourse for love so it will be more enjoyable under those circumstances. The intensity of the pleasure involved in making love is, by this standard, not the issue. Lovers do not make love simply to achieve or produce rich sensation but because they love each other. They do not love for the sake of achieving orgasm, but achieving orgasm is fully appropriate between them because they love. Indeed because they know and trust each other fully, they may hope to find in their love-making a personal fulfillment and joy that no other setting for sexual intercourse could provide.

Even marriage, therefore, is less a justification of sexual relations than is real love. Can one compare the human quality of the sexual relations between two genuinely loving but unmarried people with that of a couple married but long since out of love? No vows of yesteryear, no yellowing document can legitimate intercourse if a genuine human relationship is not present. Thus it is love, not mere mutual consent or the formality of marriage, which in this view, is the critical factor sanctioning sexual relations.

Contemporary religious thinkers who speak of a new sexual morality seem to be calling for precisely such a love ethic for intercourse. Yet some of the strongest advocates of freedom from all rules governing proper action between persons then insist that marriage is the only proper place for intercourse. Such unexpected and relatively unexplained shifts from personal to institutional standards are found in Bishop John A. T. Robinson's *Honest to God* and *Christian Morals Today*, as well as in Douglas Rhymes's perversely titled volume *No New Morality*. Richard F. Hettlinger has supplied something of the missing argument in *Living with Sex*. He asserts the lasting significance of the first intercourse, the close relation between body and self, and the indivisibility of sexuality from the general context of reproduction. Yet he can understand exceptions to that counsel and suggests certain questions that might help a couple determine if they are classed within that category. Reinhold Niebuhr and Harvey Cox have refused to accept an ethic of love-situations as adequate to the realities of human nature and the guidance of Christian wisdom. Yet they recognize that a changing society and a better understanding of sexuality require a more open sexual ethic. Hence they have proposed as a reasonable compromise that intercourse between engaged couples be legitimated. Most religious writers, however, defend the marriage standard on a prudential basis. Evelyn Millis Duvall's *Why Wait Till Marriage?* is the most persuasive discussion of the many problems standing in the way of meaningful sexual relations before marriage, probably because she is equally sensitive to the human realities involved and to traditional religious strictures. Mrs. Duvall's position brings us to the fourth and final position in the range of contemporary sexual ethics.

The advocates of the marriage ethic would not disagree with the high value placed on sexuality, mutual consent, and love. Marriage is a union based on free acceptance founded in love. There are, however, many degrees of love. Only the most significant love should be the setting for intercourse. No one can easily say how true love is to be distinguished from the many infatuations men may have, but the deepest love would be one in which two lives were so inseparably linked to one another, that they would want to share the future. Because of the unique importance of such a decision, those who would make it are asked to do so within the dignity of a social form and in terms of their deepest beliefs. Such public vows cannot guarantee anything, particularly regarding the genuineness or durability of the love—a fact which explains why many traditions, such as Judaism, allowed for divorce. Instead, by these solemnities society hoped to keep the partners from identifying a possibly temporary romance with a love that united two lives fully and "forever." It also hoped to give the partners a sense of the serious obligations they were undertaking as the corollary to this great joy of life together.

The ultimate in interpersonal acts should legitimately take place only as part of the ultimate relationship. Sexual inter-

course is an act capable of producing a life. That fact sets it apart
and endows it with a significance possessed by no other human
act. Contraception may have separated intercourse from procreation. It has not thereby changed the uniqueness of the act,
which is derived not from the bodily drives it expresses nor the
sensations it releases but from its unique potentiality.

These are four major criteria by which, it is suggested, we
might judge when sexual intercourse is right. But before we can
begin to choose between them or investigate what the Jewish
experience has been, and what it may contribute to our understanding of the issue, we must recognize that all, except the marriage standard, are based on the assumption that the girl does
not become pregnant. Accordingly, before we proceed, we must
consider the ethical implications of contraception.

4

CONTRACEPTION AS AN ETHICAL NECESSITY

IT IS ONE thing to say health, consent, or even love justifies intercourse, but it is quite another to add: even though a pregnancy
might result. Our judgment about the rightness of the act of
intercourse can hardly be separated from its consequences. Obviously, the assumption of a freer sexual morality is that there
will be no conception and that the intercourse can be judged
solely by the meaning it has for those involved in it during its
occurrence.[18] A pregnancy changes the situation radically. The
potential child must then be considered, as well as society by
virtue of its concern for all human life and particularly that of
children. Hence, if the health, consent, or love ethics are to be
accepted for what they are, there must be no pregnancy. Technically the demand is not unreasonable, given the efficiency
and availability of contraceptive devices. In actuality, however,
year after year a large number of supposedly intelligent people
continue to get involved in extramarital pregnancy. Clergymen
find themselves continually sought out by people seeking escape
from this situation. The point of this chapter is *not* that premarital intercourse is always wrong because some people become
pregnant. I am saying something quite different, namely, that
*careful, effective contraception is an ethical necessity if there is
to be any legitimation of premarital sexual intercourse.* Some
people may not accept this view. (In traditional Judaism contraception is permissible only where the woman's life is en-
dangered, or some other grave condition may result, without it.)
Other people may not care enough to prevent a pregnancy from
occurring. Hence, it is important to examine the ethical issues
posed by the various alternatives to such conscientious contraception.

21

If the couple has permitted a pregnancy to occur, they have three alternatives: marriage, abortion, or letting the child be born and placed for adoption.

All of these choices seem ethically undesirable, at worst dangerous. According to the judgment of the team from the Group for the Advancement of Psychiatry (hereafter: GAP), which studied the problem of college sex standards, "Although attitudes toward premarital sexual relations vary it can be stated unequivocally that premarital pregnancy during the college years is usually a serious if not disruptively disastrous event," and "Although in some situations it can be a maturing experience, it is one of those human dilemmas for which there is no satisfactory solution." [19]

Traditional advice to a young couple in this situation is to marry—a course then described as "doing right by her." Indeed, many a couple has an agreement to marry if a pregnancy results, and the pregnant bride is not an uncommon sight.

A moment's reflection is in order. No subject is as likely to be clouded by illusion and self-deception as sex. Realism requires this warning: the male before orgasm is eager, willing, and quick to make rash promises. Afterward, he is relaxed, calm, and able to take a long-range view of things. Besides, he becomes truly involved only if they marry. Otherwise she, not he, will undergo the abortion or bear the child. Similarly, the romanticism of the female before an unforeseen pregnancy may be far removed from the realism induced after it occurs. Does she really love him enough to want to share her life with him? Conversely, did she perhaps become pregnant so as to trap him, to wound her parents, or inflict punishment on herself?

Let us, however, grant the couple honest motivation and assume they meant what they said. Is marriage because of pregnancy an ethically acceptable substitute for proficient contraception during intercourse? Since marriage is the most important human relationship man can have, it should be entered as an act of the most mature freedom. That is why we look down on people who marry for money, position, or simply not to be left out while everyone else is doing it. These are actions involving once again barter, not freedom. The marriage of our pregnant friends is far more ethical, but it hardly proceeds from free choice. In a sterner day it was picturesquely termed a "shotgun wedding." The father and his gun are gone, the coercion remains. Ethically they cannot be said to be giving their pledges to each other of their own free will and accord. This does not mean that they will not be happy together or that their family relationships will be twisted. It is only to say that ethically this is a poor way to enter marriage.[20] Marriage is not easy even under the best circumstances. People change as they grow. New circumstances make us different. What was hidden emerges, what was latent becomes manifest. Despite the joys and exultation, the tensions and frustrations build. The achievement of a continuing love in marriage is a rare and difficult thing. In our culture, moreover, marriage is under special strains. Whether it is owing to affluence, thrill seeking, the idolization of freedom, the loss of a sense of duty or simply of respect for the married state, a good, lasting marriage has become harder to achieve. Therefore, it should be entered with every possible positive aid to its potential success.

Pregnancy is not such an aid, for it means that not only the marriage but the child comes too soon. The baby is a great joy, but he is also profoundly demanding, and he must in his dependency become the pivot around which their entire lives move. Most couples today prefer to build their personal relationship soundly before they have a child. But in this case there is no time, for marriage and family become synonymous and the problems in working for a successful marriage are compounded.

And what of the child? He, too, is entering a difficult state— life. He, too, needs the best situation possible—the full acceptance and love of his parents. It is hardly advantageous for him to have to represent unconsciously to his parents the marriage that came too soon. He and they may well overcome that handicap. Still, ethically, if we have the choice in advance, how can we remain responsible and still use it to make things more difficult for ourselves and the child?

Marriage after pregnancy is ethically far inferior to the responsible practice of contraception before.

If the couple elects the other options—abortion or bearing the child—the woman bears most of the burden. She experiences the pain of the operation or the delivery and must live directly with the guilt of ending her pregnancy or giving up her child. The shame that family and society still today attach to either course is more hers than his. Moreover, there is the risk of life, for while "only" a few women out of a thousand die in childbirth, and somewhat higher numbers after an abortion, this fact is not to be ignored in an ethical discussion. What began as an act of equal participation and responsibility has now become the woman's special burden to compensate. No decent man should put a woman he has any regard for in such a position. No woman with any self-respect should ignore her special concern with the proper practice of contraception.

Where marriage does not occur, abortion is the more likely alternative to bearing the child. It is not a simple surgical operation, such as cutting out an ingrown toenail or removing a small cyst. Abortion involves the most private organs and functions of the person. If sexuality is essential to self, then abortion must have its effect on the mother. The pregnancy ends. The scars will remain. As the GAP report puts it, "For an unmarried girl, the destruction of the fetus is an overwhelming reality about which she may sooner or later become deeply concerned. Much has been written about the possible emotional effects of the furtive and sordid atmosphere in which illegal abortions are performed; in practice we observe that the traumatic results of a legal abortion are not necessarily less severe than those of a criminal one." [21] To make abortion a casual experience is to turn the creation or termination of persons into a relatively mechanical affair. This is in odd contrast to the argument that sexuality is so central to personal existence, that intercourse ought to be freer. The person so hardened as not to care about an abortion is already less a person.

The fetus itself bears some consideration. This collection of cells is not merely that. It is alive in a way unlike any organ of the body. It might be a person. To destroy it is to infringe upon the realm of human existence. Though Jewish law permitted abortion when the mother's life or, according to some, her mental health was at stake, it could not, out of respect for life, consider abortion as anything less than an emergency procedure.[22] In the modern world, despite some recent signs of concern for the underprivileged, it is difficult not to see an erosion of concern for life. Our politics takes it for granted, and our urban way of life depends on it. I do not see how people who care about life can ethically justify doing more, even privately, to whittle away our sense of the worth of life. Nor can I see how they can disregard the fact that abortion is illegal and therefore tends to be a physically dangerous and emotionally sordid experience. Again the ethical point is that an abortion after pregnancy is no substitute for planned contraception during intercourse.

For the girl to bear the child—the third possibility—seems even less easy. Children are often born out of wedlock because their parents waited too long to have an abortion or did not have the social sophistication or economic means to carry it through. Most women seem to feel that an abortion will be less psychologically damaging than bearing a child full-term and then giving it up. Again GAP is explicit: "The student must face the fact that she is going to feel guilt, sadness and deprivation when she gives up the baby, particularly a first-born child, the one that really initiates her into biological motherhood." [23] To keep the child herself is no better a solution for many social, psychological, and ethical reasons. Doesn't the child himself desire a better start in life than this abnormal situation? Of course, he may overcome it with the help of loving, adoptive parents, but it still does not give anyone the ethical right to place him under the handicap of birth outside of marriage. Bearing an illegitimate child is no substitute ethically for the careful practice of contraception during intercourse.

I keep emphasizing this point for a very simple reason: a large number of supposedly intelligent girls turn up pregnant. Oddly enough, the problem seems to have increased since contraceptives for women have become readily available and widely publicized. When only contraceptives for the male were generally in use, it was assumed he would take care of contraception. Now, since women have reasonably easy access to the pill or the diaphragm, the male has no special responsibility for contraception, not even, it would seem, to the point of inquiring. If a woman, being a free adult, wants to have intercourse, then she should take the necessary precautions to protect herself from conceiving. This understanding is, of course, physically more inviting to the male. If a woman is either unprepared or too shy to mention the fact, pregnancy may result.

If contraception is the ethical prerequisite to any justified premarital sexual intercourse, then the male is never entitled to assume his partner has taken care of it. Too much is at stake for him to be passive. He either must use a contraceptive or make certain that his partner is using one. If he does not have that much concern for the girl who may conceive his child, he should not be sleeping with her. Her duty is no less real and certainly more urgent. What is unpardonable is that either or both parties should be too embarrassed to mention it. If they are willing to share as much physical and spiritual intimacy with one another as man can regularly know, should they not also be expected to be certain they are protected? People who consent to intercourse should be able to talk together about what they are involved in—and they have an ethical obligation to do so.

Seduction is unethical precisely because it does not allow the seduced to stop and think. Any interruption might bring back the old inhibitions. Quite tragically a good many unmarried pregnancies result from the unexpected capitulation of the delaying partner and the resultant headlong rush into intercourse without contraception.

Some people argue that contraception is wrong in principle because it introduces an element of premeditation into sexual relations that contradicts the intense, spontaneous feelings of the partners that might justify it in the first place. There is some measure of truth in this. The male must procure contraceptives. The girl who is taking birth control pills or uses a diaphragm must at some time have had the courage to see a doctor for a prescription or instructions. This seems to commit them in advance to the act. To ask the couple to interrupt their sexual pleasure for the exigencies of contraception is to intrude upon the sublimely personal with an impersonal, mechanical act. It breaks the context. It disturbs the real and significant.

One can understand this feeling. Yet its ethical worth can best be estimated by examining the alternatives it might validate. One possibility is the rhythm method, the other, simply to trust it won't happen. Both have their advocates.

Research into the cycle of female ovulation has reasonably well established that there are several days of infertility in each month. By keeping a record of the periodicity of her menstruation and by observing the changes in her body temperature, a woman can determine the time of the onset of ovulation and thus when she is infertile. The great virtue of this system is its naturalness. The partners can have the special pleasure of being in harmony with the natural flow of fertility and infertility in the female body. There is no need to trouble about contraceptives. Personal expression for one another can be fully direct and immediate.

Two decisive objections may be raised to this suggestion. First, the rhythm method is, in effect, more artificial to human lovemaking than mechanical or chemical contraception. True, it gives full freedom on certain days, but most of the time the calendar precludes it if one does not wish to have children. One distinction between men and animals is the absence of naturally prescribed occasions for intercourse. Our feelings of love do not rise and fall with the calendar. We love freely and want to express our love freely.

Adding to the artificiality is the fact that even the few infertile days are not known without substantial and careful planning by the woman. Since her ovulatory cycle may change abruptly by dint of the many chemical and psychological factors that influence her sexuality, she will have to make cycle-watching, which generally means temperature-taking, a regular part of her life. That is far more demanding than the pill.

Second, rhythm is notoriously unreliable. Despite its success with some women, there is simply no comparison between it and other methods. With equal care, the rhythm method does not work for many people much of the time, while mechanical contraceptives work for almost all of the people all the time. (This explains much of the current agitation in the Roman Catholic church for a change in its understanding of ethical birth control. Many Catholics are, in fact, using contraceptive devices in violation of the norm taught by their church—reasserted in the recent papal encyclical *Humanae vitae*—justifying it as fidelity to conscience.)[24]

Thus while the modern technology of contraception does somewhat interrupt the free interpersonal movement to intercourse, I must conclude that, because of the risk of pregnancy, it is far more ethical to employ contraceptives than to use the rhythm method. Indeed, I consider the risk of an unwanted pregnancy resulting from the rhythm method so great that I believe it unethical even for married couples to use it.[25]

One further possibility remains. Some couples do not want the obligation of thinking about all this or of taking the responsibility of preventing conception. Consequently, they have intercourse and trust to luck. They know some days are infertile, some are not, and some people get by for quite a while this way. When people are in such a romantic mood, it is no time for argument. Things are so good, the world is so right, everything should conform to this inner experience. Romance is beautiful because for a moment our emotions seem fully capable of ruling the world. To lose the capacity for romance is to lose much of what it means to be a man. Yet to insist on bending reality to our own sentiments is to open ourselves to disillusion and despair. That is a major reason we have so many divorces today. We think we love enough to marry, but it turns out we are only interested in prolonged romance. The day-to-day confrontation of life in a real world might be met through love, but it cannot provide us with endless romance.

If two people care for one another enough to express their feelings in sexual intercourse, they should care enough *not* to have a child casually or by accident, insofar as they can help it.

To say the use of a contraceptive may break a mood strikes me as an odd counterargument. Anyone who is so anxious to protect his mood must be using his emotion as a defense. He is probably doubtful that the intercourse is right, and he can only overcome that doubt by immersing himself in feeling. Contraception under these circumstances would entail taking responsibility for the act. Yet, although allowing romance the ascendancy relieves him of having to decide anything, the very abandonment of control opens the door to greater evils.[26]

Worse, Freud taught us there are no mistakes, only the expression of unconscious desires. He also taught us there is more sexual energy in our unconscious than our conscious selves can perceive. One does not have to be an orthodox Freudian to understand why there are always a certain number of people, married and unmarried, who claim to have used contraceptives, yet have unwanted pregnancies. Some of them may be traced to chemical causes or faulty contraceptives. Yet the pregnancy statistics are greater than such infrequent possibilities. It is far more likely that one or both partners unconsciously wanted to have children. Their contraception failed because they unconsciously but effectively caused it to fail. Understanding that and knowing how the unconscious mind works do not stop it from making itself felt. Hence, anyone who wishes to avoid pregnancy must examine his conscious mind with great care and attention, which means getting reliable information about contraception and not depending on supposedly informed or experienced friends. It means knowing how to use the devices properly and receiving authoritative answers to any questions concerning them. Fortunately many college health services or doctors near campuses will provide such help readily to any mature inquirer. And, of course, it means making certain someone is employing a contraceptive before intercourse begins.

I understand the ethical imperative as follows: if you think it could be right to have premarital sexual intercourse, you must insist that it can be carried out only when it is reasonably certain there will be no pregnancy. Premarital sexual intercourse *without* contraception is by that fact alone unethical. Further-

more, such contraception must be practiced carefully and con-
scientiously. Only on that condition is it possible that their will
to intercourse might be adjudged ethical.

We can now turn to a detailed analysis of each of the four
proposed standards of sexual practice. Our study of them will
concentrate on the values which each embodies. By our agreement or disagreement with these values, we can choose the most
acceptable ethic. To sensitize us to the interrelations of values
and standards and to give us the historic experience of a group
that has tried various forms in pursuit of its ideals, we will look
first at the record of the Jewish people.

5

THE JEWISH EXPERIENCE

JUDAISM CONSIDERS sex God's gift and procreation His command.[27] It considers marriage the proper context for intercourse and makes it a prescribed religious duty. With such a high value given to marriage,[28] Judaism would thus seem to side with those who see it as the necessary condition for sexual intercourse. Yet neither the Torah, the rest of the Bible, the Mishnah, nor the Talmud contains a law prohibiting premarital sexual relations. In clarifying this paradox one can learn a good deal about Jewish tradition as well as about the problem of sexual standards.

Let us begin with the biblical data. The Torah prohibits adultery, incest, selling one's daughter into prostitution, and the rape or seduction of a betrothed maiden. Each is a case of sexual relations involving people in a special situation: married or pledged to be married; members of a family; or available for payment. None of them deals directly with our question. There are, however, two laws which tell us of the penalties involved when a girl not betrothed has been raped or seduced. They may be rendered as follows:

> If a man seduces a virgin who has not been betrothed and he has intercourse with her, he must make her his wife by paying the bride-price to her father. If her father, for whatever reasons of his own, refuses to give the girl to him, the man must still pay the father the bride-price for virgins (Exod. 22:15-16).

> If a man comes upon a virgin who is not betrothed, seizes her and has intercourse with her and they are discovered, the rapist shall pay the girl's father fifty shekels of silver and she shall be his wife. Moreover, because the man violated her he can never have the right to divorce her (Deut. 22:28-29).

The reading of these laws carries us back three thousand years or more. They move in the spirit of other ancient Near Eastern legislation of the time. For purposes of adjudicating the rights involved, the law is addressed only to the men. The one inflicts the damage and now must pay for it. The other, the father, receives the payment and, in the case of seduction, determines whether his daughter shall marry this man or not. On this level of claim and damage, the Exodus-Deuteronomy legislation attaches no special onus to seduction. Its concern is right and compensation, not what we would call the "ethics" of the situation. Sometimes ethical judgments are explicitly given in the laws of the Torah. Here none is stated. Let the man marry her, and as far as the damages are concerned, the matter is concluded. It almost seems as if the father is the aggrieved party in the rape or seduction, since his daughter, whose virginity has been taken, will now bring him a lesser bride-price, if indeed he can succeed in marrying her off at all. The girl hardly comes into the case because she is not yet, at this stage of Jewish legal development, regarded as a competent legal entity. Her father is responsible for her. Hence, her rights are expressed in terms of his—all of which provided the impulse for later changes in Jewish law and, indirectly, the modern fight for the emancipation of women.

This presentation alone should make clear that one cannot speak of Judaism simply as a religion of law. To know the commandments alone is not yet to know Judaism, especially if one does not know the biblical law in terms of its rabbinic development. Even then one only has a beginning. Christian interpreters of Judaism often overstress the place of law in Judaism because they wish to argue that Jewish legalism, Pharisaism as they see it, is inferior to Christianity's religion of love. Jews, too, often insist Judaism is primarily a religion of law because they want to fight the I'll-do-as-I-please attitude of modern acculturated Jews.[29] Like many exaggerations these views are founded on a partial truth. The law is central to Judaism, but it arises in a context of what modern men would call ethical concerns and religious beliefs and is practiced in a real community in a given area at a given time. The law must always be understood in terms of the belief and practice of the community. They not only give it its effective meaning but are a major means of changing the law itself as time goes on.

Similarly, in relation to sex there are a good deal of these wider data in the Bible, but they are not very detailed or unambiguous.[30] Perhaps the most important thing to be noted is the general attitude toward sexuality that permeated the community and its spiritual traditions. Its God transcends sexuality and is antiorgiastic, in contrast to the gods of surrounding peoples. He establishes the standards for human sexuality rather than represents its ideal.[31] The early Hebrews knew He created man to live in family units. His first commandments to Adam is "be fruitful and multiply." [32] Sexual activity is considered part of Adam's pure existence in the Garden of Eden previous to his sin. Sex itself and procreation are divine and good. When woman is created to give the lonely Adam a helpmate who is "bone of my bones and flesh of my flesh," the Torah text comments, "Therefore a man shall leave his father and mother and cleave to his wife so that they become one flesh" (Gen. 2:23, 24). Sexuality completes the person. Man and wife are the model of integrated humanity.

The lives of most of the great men in the Bible reflect this sentiment. Though polygamy is permitted, it is not often practiced after the founding of the monarchy, and then mostly by the nobility. The biblical heroes are generally monogamous and do not seem discontent with only one wife. To the Judaic mind their heroism did not lie in their sexual feats, amazingly demonstrated. The Bible knows sex and loves children, but it does not consider sexual prowess the source of true masculinity. It affirms the importance of the family, so that adultery is considered a fearful sin. Again and again the Bible uses it as the symbol of indecency and degeneration. The law, following ancient Semitic practice, defines adultery only in terms of a married woman's intercourse with anyone other than her husband, or in terms of any man's intercourse, whether he is married or not, with a married woman not his wife. This is far narrower than the modern sense of the term. In these legal strictures, we can see the broad outlines of monogomous marriage as the basis of family solidarity emerging in biblical Judaism.

Two further emphases tend, though again by indirect means, to make marriage the ideal for sexual relations. The first is the high value placed on bridal virginity. The Bible so closely connects being a girl with sexual purity, that it simply calls her a virgin. It often refers to virginity in the most laudatory terms. Yet virginity is given no worth in itself, as a state to be preserved. When Jepthah's daughter was to be sacrificed, she and her friends bewailed her unmarried, virgin state, and bewailing virginity unfulfilled in marriage and children was apparently an annual rite.[33] Virginity was the community standard for desirable wives. Thus, there is a legal provision that a groom whose wife turns out not to be a virgin has the right to demand the return of his bride-price.[34] Fathers were obviously concerned, for legal as well as social and ethical reasons, to see to it that their daughters remained virgins until marriage.

With unmarried women guarded or on guard and married women strongly protected by the law of adultery, the chief form of sexual promiscuity in biblical times was prostitution. Here too there is no direct law against a man, married or unmarried, visiting a prostitute, though there is a law against giving one's daughter into prostitution. This is assumed to be one of those cases where the Torah does not bother to prohibit specifically that which everyone's conscience should proscribe.[35] The Bible mentions prostitution as one fact among the many other harsh realities of human existence and often treats it with simple objectivity. Yet when the prophets judge Israel's behavior or the poets seek figures to describe falseness and wickedness, to go whoring is a frequent image of spiritual degradation and corruption.

In the Bible, then, there is a delicate balance in the attitude toward sexuality. On the one hand, it is natural, created, commanded, joyful. On the other, it is the most common symbol of the broader human problems of temptation and the transgression of God's law. These are easy to understand when presented in sexual terms because sexual sin is so common and so powerful an experience. Hence, the Bible condemns sexual immorality both as an evil in itself and as a model of human sinfulness. It also uses woman's sexual fidelity in marriage as a major symbol of man's proper relationship to God. So sex is both man's blessing and his problem, his nature and his opportunity, his downfall and his fulfillment.

For all its interest, the Bible does not give us very direct help with the ethics of premarital intercourse. Its guidance is oblique: virginity is prized, but nonvirgins can marry without stigma, and someone who wants to marry a nonvirgin is free to do so. Sexuality is honorable and to be fulfilled in marriage, but there is no direct law or explicit statement against premarital sexual intercourse.

The truth of the matter would seem to be, as the later data of the rabbinic period make quite clear, that we fail to obtain a clear-cut response because our inquiry emerges from an entirely different social setting. We tend to marry in our twenties or, because of schooling, military service, or other factors, even later. This prolongs the period after puberty during which the problem of premarital sexual activity must be dealt with. Biblical Jewry knew no such extended gestation into adulthood. There was little or no formal schooling, labor was needed, and life was short. People probably married early, and more important for our purposes, their marriages were arranged long before actually taking place. Since there are not many accounts in the Bible of matchmaking and marriage, and even fewer laws regarding them, we shall have to turn to rabbinic times. Much of the material we have was put into its present form during the first century C.E. It undoubtedly reflects the general patterns of what had been going on for some time, though exactly how far back into biblical times this or that detail may be traced is, as usual, a matter of academic argument.

The major data for our discussion are provided by rabbinic law dealing with the ages of a girl and her legal rights relative to marriage. An early tradition, fixed before the specific ages were set, puts the distinction this way:

The sages compared the stages in a woman's development to those of a fig, which has three—unripe, ripening, and ripe. Unripe is the equivalent of her being yet a child, while ripening is the equivalent of her maidenhood. In both stages her father has a legal right to possess anything she may find or produce by her work and to annul her vows. She is like a ripe fig when she matures, and then her father no longer has authority over her. What are the visible signs that she has reached maturity? R. Jose the Galilean said, "When a wrinkle appears under the breast." R. Akiba said, "When the breasts hang down." R. Ben Azzai said, "When the ring around the nipple darkens." R. Jose said, "When the breasts are so developed that, should a hand be placed on the tip of a nipple, it sinks and only slowly rises again." [36]

The rabbis thus define three stages in her maturation.[37] In each of these definitions they quite self-consciously give her more and more status as a person under the law. As long as a girl is not yet twelve years of age, she remains fully under her father's jurisdiction. Between twelve and twelve and a half she is technically a maiden, a *naarah,* and though still essentially under her father's jurisdiction, she has the special responsibilities which the Torah laws impose on one involved in seduction, especially should she be betrothed.[38] At twelve and a half she becomes a *bogeret,* a "mature one," legally competent to act for herself in relation to marriage and other matters.[39]

While fathers were discouraged from making matches for daughters under twelve, the practice was not uncommon.[40] The prime time for matchmaking was in her period of *naarah,* from age twelve to twelve and a half. She was then old enough to be a conscious party to the match and to allow the husband's father to have some idea of her physical appearance as an adult. If her father had not concluded an agreement for her by the time she was twelve and a half, she became a *bogeret,* and he technically no longer had the power to contract a marriage for her and collect the bride-price (though in practice it was generally no longer given). More important, the laws of the Torah concerning the seduction and rape of a virgin were understood as applying only to the *naarah*. The *bogeret*, the girl of over twelve and a half years of age, was now enough of a legal personality to be considered responsible for her own sexual behavior without benefit of special legal protection. If she wanted to take the risks of intercourse and loss of virginity, it was not the law's concern. It gave her no claim against a seducer, and a man marrying a *bogeret* could not bring a charge against her that she was not a virgin.[41] No wonder the other term occasionally used for such a woman is *penuyah*, which means literally "a free one." She was free under the law (at twelve and a half) to act in sexual matters by her own decision, but she was also without any legal remedies should someone take sexual advantage of her. A girl's father was obviously under strong pressure to make a match for his daughter before she became a *bogeret*. The following is a characteristic statement:

> There is an authoritative tradition concerning two interpretations of the verse, "Do not profane your daughter by making her a whore" (Lev. 19:29). R. Eliezer said, "This refers to one who marries his young daughter to an old man. That is bound to lead to trouble." R. Akiba said, "This refers to one who delays marrying off his daughter so that she becomes a *bogeret*."
>
> In this connection a somewhat odd statement attributed by R. Kahana to R. Akiba is of interest: "The only poor Jews are either those who are subtle about their wickedness or who delay marrying off their daughters so that they reach the stage of *bogeret*." What is odd is that the two cases are the same, for a man who is subtle about his wickedness is precisely one who delays marrying off his daughter. That was why R. Abaye read the statement this way: "What poor Jew is subtle about his wickedness? He who delays marrying off his daughter so that she becomes a *bogeret*. . . ."
>
> An anonymous tradition applies the following verse to a man who marries off his children when they attain puberty: "You shall know your tent is peaceful; you shall take stock of your dwelling and not find sin" (Job 5:24).[42]

Marriage by the late teens after a much earlier betrothal was apparently the general custom in rabbinic times,[43] and with some variation, it continued well into medieval times.[44] The

critical point, however, is that once the girl is betrothed, intercourse between her and any Jew except her husband-to-be (an act
regarded as immoral, though not specifically prohibited by law)
was considered adultery.[45] "Engagement," then, was a sort of semi-
marriage, by modern standards. It specifically prohibited, with
the full force of the Torah's ban against adultery, sexual relations
with any other man. Until modern times this was undoubtedly
the major means by which the Jewish community met the problem of premarital sexual relations.[46] Jewish children were prom-
ised in marriage at an early age, and they knew that this was to be
one of the most important facts of their lives. This knowledge
tended to keep them chaste, even as early marriage soon gave
them sexual release. Moreover, adultery was so serious a sin and
the legal penalties attached to it so great, that there were strong
prudential reasons for betrothed girls to avoid premarital intercourse. All this reflected widespread community feeling and was
reinforced by social pressure. These interlocking sanctions and
ideals shaped the practice of the Jewish community until relatively recent times and did so with that ennobling of sexuality
through marriage that has been so notable a part of the history
of the Jews.

This discussion has not yet answered the question of the per-
missibility of premarital sexual intercourse today. What about
those who do not marry young? What might rabbinic authorities say about those who must, like many modern youths, wait
until their twenties to marry?

Under the system of early betrothal, with the full penalty of
adultery attached to it, premarital intercourse by unengaged
adults was not a common problem. Either because of its rarity or
because they considered this matter best left in the sphere of personal ethical decision, the rabbis made no direct prohibition
against it. The legal rights of the *bogeret* (at twelve and a half)
to engage in intercourse seem clear, technically, and the male
has even more freedom to do so. The rabbis, however, would
seem to consider it immoral, though even here clear-cut statements are not readily available. The following statement from
the Talmud is about as specific as the rabbis ever get:

Rav Judah said Rav [third-century Babylonian master] once related the following incident: A man conceived a passion for a certain woman, and his heart was so consumed by this burning desire, he seemed likely to die. When doctors were consulted, they said, "His only cure is to have intercourse with her." The sages then ruled that rather than compel her to have intercourse with him, let him die. The doctors said, "Then let her stand nude before him." The sages said, "Better he should die than that she should be made to stand nude before him." The doctors said, "At least let her talk to him, even from behind a fence." The sages were adamant, "Rather than make her talk with him, even from behind a fence, let him face dying."

This attitude of the sages caused a difference of opinion between R. Jacob ben Idi, and R. Samuel ben Nahmani. The one said they ruled in this way because she was a married woman. The other said she was not. Now it would be clear why they would be so strict if she were married, but what would be the reason if she were unmarried? R. Papa said, "Because of the blot this would bring on her family name." R. Aha ben Ika said, "So that Jewish girls might have no pretext for becoming morally dissolute by having even so unnatural a case as an example of sanctioned sexual immorality." Then the sages should have suggested that he simply marry her. That would not have assuaged his passion, as we have learned from R. Isaac, who said, "Since the day the Temple was destroyed, the full pleasure of sexual intercourse has been taken away from the moral and given only to those who sin; as Scripture says, 'Stolen waters are sweet, and bread eaten in secret is pleasant'" (Prov. 9:17).[47]

In sexual matters, the rabbis were primarily concerned with condemning the prevalent immoralities of their day—adultery and prostitution.[48] Their references to sexual immorality or licentiousness in general must be presumed [49] to refer to these acts rather than to premarital intercourse.[50] The same is true of medieval rabbinic literature. We cannot easily discern the actual facts in most cases because the sages regularly use euphemisms when discussing sexual matters so as to avoid unclean speech. Yet the general attitude toward premarital intercourse may be inferred from the indirect controls created in the first centuries

C.E to prevent any sexual relations but those of a married couple.

The rabbis went far beyond the biblical safeguards to sexuality. They too esteemed virginity highly and sought to protect it by elaborating a stringent set of standards for female modesty.[51] Women, particularly young women, were expected to spend most of their time in the confines of their homes. When they ventured out, they were expected to be dressed so that no part of their body showed. They probably wore veils and some sort of head covering so that their hair, which was considered sexually arousing, should not be seen. When women had to be present in public, such as at the synagogue, at weddings, or at funerals, provision was made to segregate them. On the other hand, males were warned not to have too much to do with women, they were generally forbidden to be alone with them or visit them socially without chaperones, and they were advised, if they wanted to be scrupulous in their behavior, not to touch them or even look at them. While a good many of these and related provisions changed with the times—and the more severe restrictions applied only to the most pious of the community— the general sense of this effort to avoid contact between the sexes remained constant in Jewish practice over the centuries. Sephardic Jews under Arabic rule have tended to maintain them down to the present, though Ashkenazi Jews, under the influence of freer European customs, had already begun liberalizing these practices by the eighteenth century.

The effect of these laws is quite clear. They aimed not only at preventing adultery but any kind of sexual relations outside of marriage.

The rabbis reinforced these practices with their sense of the exalted worth of marriage and their warnings against the sinful power of the sexual drive. In the latter case, they go far beyond the Bible. They understand man, all his life, to be tempted by his "evil urge." This primitive life energy they know is not merely bad, for it provides the motive force by which men build, create, and procreate:

Of the verse "And behold, it was very good" (Gen. 1:3), R. Nahman ben Samuel said, "That refers to the evil urge. 'What, is the evil urge then very good?' Yes, for if not for it, men would not build a house, or take a wife, or beget a child, or engage in business. As Scripture says, 'All labor and skillful work come about because of a man's rivalry with his neighbor' " (Eccles. 4:4).[52]

Yet it is also the power which leads man into sin, sometimes by overwhelming passion, at other times, by subtle or devious devices. This evil urge is identified most closely with man's sexual impulse. Here the rabbis feel man is most easily led into sin. As a result, they are continually concerned to warn man against the power of the evil urge and to suggest remedies, most notably the study of Torah, against its enticements. Though adultery and prostitution are foremost in their minds, it is not difficult to see that premarital sexual intercourse would well come within this moral censure.

Regardless of sentimental notions about how pure Jews were in olden days, honesty compels the recognition that sexual offenses against Jewish morality occurred in every age and every community. Jewish legal and historical literature over the centuries contains numerous references to adulterers and adulteresses, and to the problems of prostitution. But they were neither typical nor common. They did not determine the ethos of the Jewish community nor effectively damage its devotion to meaningful marriage and stable families. They did not fundamentally shift its sexual attitudes toward the promiscuity common among other peoples, nor did they ever shake the Jewish community's trust that marriage was the only proper place for sexual relations. The Jews were quite human in sexual matters, but they created an extraordinary way of life in which sex was but another means of ennobling man's total existence.

In the twelfth century, however, as part of the great legal code of Maimonides, the *Mishneh Torah* ("The Torah in Review"), we suddenly discover a flat, full-scale legal prohibition against premarital sexual intercourse—followed almost immediately by an exception! Maimonides writes, at the beginning of the section entitled "Matrimony and Related Matters,"

> There are in this area four commandments, two enjoining duties, two prohibiting certain acts. Specifically, they are that (1) one should marry a woman by means of a formal contract and the rabbinically enjoined rites; (2) one should not have intercourse with a woman unless one has given her a marriage contract and performed the appropriate marriage rites. . . .

He goes into greater detail in the chapter which immediately follows:

> Before the time of the giving of the Torah, if a man met a woman in the street and they were both agreeable, he would give her her price, and they would have intercourse at the road-side, after which he went his way. This is what the Torah means when it speaks of the woman it calls a *kedeshah*. However, once the Torah was given, the *kedeshah* was forbidden, as it is written, "No Israelite woman shall be a *kedeshah*" (Deut. 23:18). There-fore, anyone who has casual intercourse with a woman is to be punished at the order of the Jewish community court for the transgression of this commandment of the Torah, since he had intercourse with a *kedeshah*.[53]

In this statement of Maimonides we may see a good deal of the legal genius which aroused at once the admiration and the ire of the contemporary Jewish scholarly world. All the rabbinic tradition which we have labored to clarify, Maimonides sum-marizes in one short paragraph. What was unclear, he makes precise and definite. What was implicit or only indirectly treated by the various authorities, he makes explicit and in a simple and forthright way. Though no one before him had ever stated the law this way, none of his later antagonists ever argues that Maimonides has not correctly stated its general position cor-rectly. Maimonides did that again and again, covering every area of Jewish law, the theoretical as well as the practical, creat-ing the first systematic code of all the legal traditions down to his time.

His legal construction here is quite ingenious. Maimonides

bases his ruling on the law prohibiting the *kedeshah*. Modern scholarship, basing itself on comparative Semitic usages, defines the term as "cult prostitute." [54] Thus Israel, in direct contrast to its neighbors, is prohibited from having religious prostitutes as an adjunct to the service of its God. So successful was the law, that later Jewish tradition is oblivious even of the existence of such a possibility. Normal rabbinic usage seemed to consider the term *kedeshah* another word for "prostitute," though some rabbis understood it as meaning a slave acquired for sexual purposes.[55] While the exact meaning of the prohibition in the Torah is therefore not completely clear, it is obviously related to sexual immorality. Maimonides utilizes it as the authority for barring all unmarried intercourse. Had he used a verse relating to the usual prostitute, the *zonah,* he would have been limited to cases where payment is involved. Had he found a way around that, he might have made all women involved in nonmarital sexual relations come under the *zonah* category and thus become involved in the problems which would arise if they were to marry into a priestly family. By basing his ruling on the *kedeshah* commandment (a step well within the limits of Jewish legal interpretation), he had found specific legal authority for what was the spirit of the Jewish tradition, without limiting the ultimate marital possibilities of the women involved.[56] On this point, too, most commentators did not argue with him.

The disagreement came over what many of the authorities felt was the one legitimate exception to the rule—the *pilegesh,* normally translated as "concubine," a topic that is not only intriguing but highly relevant to our contemporary question. Let us briefly trace the background.

Many great biblical figures had concubines. Abraham had Hagar, and Jacob had Bilhah and Zilpah. Saul had at least one, David, ten, and Solomon, 300. Lesser men also apparently had concubines, as the stories in the Book of Judges indicate. They were not wives in the fullest sense, but they obviously had a socially recognized, respected, familial relation to their men.[57] We do not hear much of them in later biblical or rabbinic times, though there was some practice of polygamy.[58] The references to the *pilegesh* in the Talmud are more a matter of theory than practice.[59] The major one concerns the meaning of the biblical terms:

> What are "wives" and what are "concubines"? Rav Judah said that Rav had taught that wives have a marriage contract and were taken by the accepted rabbinic rites. Concubines have no contract and came to live with their man without benefit of ceremony.[60]

Rav does not reject the institution but by defining it permits, theoretically at least, a relation in which a man and woman live together even though they are not formally married. Considering the biblical precedent, it is difficult to see how he could have done otherwise. Centuries later, however, Maimonides was far more stringent. He prohibited all sexual relations unless, specifically, there was a contract and the rites. He certainly knew the traditions concerning the *pilegesh*, but he permitted her only to a king.[61] It is not unfair to charge him with being generally repressive in sexual matters, since, as an Aristotelian, he accepted the denigration of the body for the sake of exalting mind and thought.[62]

With respect to concubinage, Maimonides went too far, and the democracy of Jewish learning speedily asserted itself against him. Even in his own day the other legal masters challenged the validity of his ruling on the *pilegesh*, and modern editions of Maimonides' code print their objections crowding around his ruling in eternal disputatious commentary. His classic antagonist and contemporary, Rabbi Abraham ben David (1120-1198) of Posquieres, France, has this note to the Maimonidean ruling:

> The term *kedeshah* surely denotes a woman who is prepared for sexual relations and makes herself available to all men. However, a woman who gives herself exclusively to one man is not liable to punishment at the order of the Jewish communal court, nor does she transgress any prohibition of Jewish law, for she is a *pilegesh*, a concubine, of the kind mentioned in the Bible. The lexicographers derive the word by metathesis and combination from words meaning "for a mistress." She is available at times for intercourse and to take care of the house.

The point made here is repeated by many other commentators and becomes a matter of serious contention for the next several centuries in Jewish law. The attack is always the same: Maimonides might have been supreme in summarizing and systematizing Jewish law, but he had no right to change it or arbitrarily nullify one of its legitimate options. If the Bible permitted concubines, and did so for all Jews, then Maimonides cannot by simple fiat restrict them to kings. The concern of the commentators must be linked with the fact that concubinage had become a living reality in their times. From the literature it would seem that after centuries in which it had been unknown, it had now arisen among Spanish Jews, who were copying the style of their Moslem and Christian patrons.[63] It is also attested among other European Jews in this period and for the next several centuries, though to a far lesser degree.

The situation in all its legal, social, and moral aspects is well summarized in the formal legal response which Nahmanides (1194-1270), probably the most important scholar in the period following Maimonides, sent to his pupil Rabbi Jonah Gerondi:

> O Holy Man, Man of God, the pious rabbi, Rabbi Jonah. May your well-being and the well-being which comes from your teaching grow forever and increase ceaselessly!
>
> Your inquiry to me to make known to you in a direct and straightforward way my opinion on the question of the *pilegesh* has reached me.
>
> I do not know why people have doubts in this matter, for she is surely permitted as long as he has taken her for himself exclusively. Casual intercourse is prohibited to the Jews only on the authority of Rabbi Eliezer ben Jacob's statement that, except for such a prohibition, it might happen that a brother would marry his sister or a father, his daughter. Of such a state of affairs the Torah speaks when it says, "and the earth will be filled with immorality." But if she comes into his home and is exclusively his, then her sons are called by his name, and she is permitted to him. Thus, David married a *pilegesh*, and we do not find in the Bible or in the Talmud any distinction in this matter between a king of Israel and a commoner. Rather we find that a number of the great men of Israel "married" a con-

cubine. . . . [Caleb and Gideon are cited as examples. This is followed by a refutation of the theory that the practice was limited to leaders or considered sinful.] No, taking a *pilegesh* was permitted and practiced in Israel in biblical times. . . . And if you would argue that, though it is permitted by the Torah, it has been prohibited by rabbinic enactment, in what place is this ruling to be found in the Talmud, or what community court promulgated it, and in what era was it decreed? . . . [There follows the rejection of a possible argument from the ban against interrupted marital procedures.] But if he wants her to be his *pilegesh* so that they live together but without undertaking full legal entailments toward one another [which will mean that she is not forbidden to other men], and he therefore does not perform any marriage rites for her, why, he may do so. . . . [A somewhat ingenuous effort to square this liberality with the stricter teaching of Maimonides follows, including a brief reference to the law concerning non-Jewish maidservants.]

As for you, Rabbi Jonah our teacher, may God give you life, prohibit the *pilegesh* to the people in your community, for if they know that she is legally permitted, they will become licentious and immoral, and they will have intercourse with their women while they are still menstruous.[64]

Nahmanides boldly faces social reality and legal precedent. People are taking "concubines," who are more than mistresses yet less than wives, but Nahmanides insists they have a legal right to do so. He is, then, as compared to Maimonides, liberal with regard to the *pilegesh* relationship.[65]

For our purposes, it is interesting to see what structure he sees in this relationship. He notes the entry of the *pilegesh* into the home, her exclusive relationship to her man, and the full legitimacy of his children by her. This, apparently, is the reason why it is permitted despite Nahmanides' citation of R. Eliezer ben Jacob's rule against free sexual relations, namely, that incest might abound. He even terms the act of taking her a "marrying," though it is without contract or rites, and she is not bound by the laws concerning adultery.[66]

This closely resembles the modern ethics of mutual consent or of love, though in its semipermanent nature, it seems far more

like the latter than the former, which might well be quite temporary. So we must say that the Jewish tradition has in an earlier
period given legal sanction to certain forms of nonmarital, or,
better, semimarital, sexual relationships. That recognition or acceptance continued from biblical times through the Middle Ages,
with a varying incidence of practice until Maimonides tried to put
an end to it. He did not succeed in his own day, though ultimately his position became the standard for Jewish law.

The reason for which the *pilegesh* relationship did not remain
acceptable is already to be found in Nahmanides' *responsum:*
it might have had a precedent in ancient times, but it could no
longer be considered morally desirable. The reason Nahmanides
gives—that, if allowed, the men may have relations with women
who have not observed the laws of ritual cleanliness—seems to
me more a legal justification of the moral condemnation than a
real reason for the ruling. The Jewish moral tide was running
against concubinage, and by the first part of the fourteenth century, the two great legal authorities of the period, Asher ben
Yehiel and Jacob ben Asher, father and son, ruled against the
legitimacy of the *pilegesh*.[67] They based this not only on the
problem of menstrual intercourse but on the "blemish" a concubine brings to a family name. Their decision carried great weight
in succeeding generations, though some dissent remained.[68]
Thus, when the climactic code of Joseph Karo, the *Shulhan
Arukh* ("The Prepared Table"), was published in 1565, it could,
despite the arguments since Maimonides' time, say quite flatly:

Laws of Marriage and Related Matters

These are based on the commandment not to take a woman
as one's wife simply by having intercourse with her and the
prohibition of intercourse with an adult unmarried woman even
if a man takes her to himself for an exclusive relationship.

A woman is considered married only when she has undergone
all the prescribed marriage rites. Should a man have intercourse
with her but not with intent to marry her, this does not affect
her marital status. Even if he had intercourse with her for the
sake of marrying her thereby, but did so without indicating this
intention to witnesses, she is still not considered his wife. The

same holds true even if he took her for an exclusive relationship with himself. On the contrary, in this last case the Jewish community court may coerce him until he sends her from his house.[69]

The *Shulhan Arukh* was soon accepted as authoritative by Sephardic Jewry in the Mediterranean countries. The Europeans proper, the Ashkenazim, resisted it because it often did not reflect their practices. Yet largely because of the enthusiasm for it by the great Polish teacher and contemporary of Karo, Moses Isserles, and equally because of his comments on it, which reflected Ashkenazic custom, the *Shulhan Arukh* ultimately became the most authoritative legal work among European Jews as well. It remains to this day the fundamental law code for Ashkenazic communities wherever they have migrated. Isserles' comment on this passage is of interest, not least because it somewhat mitigates the otherwise complete negativity toward the *pilegesh:*

> For surely a woman living in this circumstance would be ashamed to go to the ritual bath to cleanse herself as the law requires, and then her man would have intercourse with her while she was still technically in the status of a menstruant. That is the reason for this prohibition as given in the code *The Four Rows* [ca. 1300]. However, if he set her aside for himself exclusively and she does go faithfully to the ritual bath, there are some authorities, like Abraham ben David of Posquieres, and a few of the commentators who permit this. She is then a *pilegesh*, of whom the Torah speaks. Others say this is always forbidden, and the Jewish community court may punish them for such a relationship on the grounds of the commandment in the Torah, "No Israelite woman shall be a *kedeshah*," and that is the opinion of Maimonides, Asher ben Yehiel, and Jacob ben Asher.

Since Maimonides and Jacob ben Asher were two of the three major voices used in determining the rulings of the *Shulhan Arukh,* the citation of the dissenting opinion must be taken more as an academic nicety than a genuine option. From the standpoint of the legal authorities the matter was as good as closed. However, one still hears in succeeding generations of the *pilegesh* relationship being practiced, and one authority of distinction, Jacob Emden (1697-1776), argues for its revival as a means of keeping his generation from greater sexual sinning.[70] Yet it is no longer a practical possibility for most of the legal authorities.[71] Moral development has made it indefensible.[72]

To some it will seem strange that what religious law once authorized might in another generation become considered a lesser standard of behavior, that, in effect, there had been growth or development in God's own law. The modern believer might put it this way: time not only brings changed social circumstances in which traditional practices can no longer operate effectively, but it can also bring new insights into what man is or what society can be or what God requires of them. The law changes to reflect them both. That is one of the important differences between a legal and a philosophic system. Law is always bound to time and place. If it is to remain effective, it must allow for change and adaptation. Philosophy, particularly the older Greek philosophies, sought for a truth that transcended time and place and was eternal. It might be known as truth by its immutability. That which must change cannot be true, until in the Hegelian dialectic the process of change in time becomes itself a disclosure of truth. Perhaps, too, the need to change explains one of the disadvantages of legal rather than philosophic thinking. Where the philosophers are strongest in giving reasons, the judges often give us only hints or snatches of why they decide as they do. If they fully disclosed their reasons, their laws would be only as good as their reasons and could not change unless their explanations did.[73] That may be why philosophy of law always seems to follow after the cases.

Judaism, deeply concerned with what mankind does in time, has for the most part preferred law to philosophy. Its legal tradition is self-consciously concerned with the need and the right to adapt the law to changing circumstances. Naturally there will be arguments over when the time for such development has come and how far it ought to go. In an emergency the rabbis could directly change or override an explicit commandment of the Torah. Until modern times, most changes took place more as a matter of slow evolution than of planned development. In either case the rabbis knew themselves authorized to teach the law for their day, and they did. As the statement oft-quoted by moderns puts it: "Whatever an experienced legal master innovates in a later age was already given to Moses at Sinai as part of the Torah." [74] The growth and development of the law is authorized by God to make possible the people of Israel's continuing faithfulness to Him in history.

Thus, as we move into the modern period, Judaism, which had for some centuries permitted the *pilegesh* relationship, rejected it. The traditional Jewish community was committed legally and morally to marriage as the only situation in which sexual intercourse should occur. While twice in recent years it has been suggested by eminent scholars that the *pilegesh* relationship might make possible a solution to certain difficult problems which arise under contemporary Jewish marriage law, the general response to them has been completely negative.[75] Complete prohibition remains, apparently, the position of the Jewish legal authorities of our day.

This does not mean modern man must reach the same conclusion. If anything, the record of Jewish experience probably shows more tolerance to nonmarital sexual relationships than most people ever believed. Yet knowing something of what the Jews have thought and done in other ages ought to give us a fresh perspective on our particular social situation, on the special contours it gives our version of the sexual problem, and on the values which are implicit in advocating one or another response to it.

The Values

6

THE ETHICS OF HEALTHY ORGASM

OFTEN, one discovers, different ethical standards arise because people hold different views about the nature of man. A good way to go about choosing a sex ethic might therefore be to begin by elucidating the attitudes toward man implicit in each of the four possibilities described in the preceding chapters. Then, when agreement is reached about the most acceptable view, one will know which to adopt and why. The ethical task therefore turns out to be as much a labor of self-discovery as of intellectual analysis. Confronted with differing estimates of what is important, one must declare his real concerns and thus his real identity. This can be so disturbing, that most people try to avoid ethical decisions. Life, however, is generally a series of compulsory choices, which is why so much of it is a painful sort of education.

We begin with the ethics of healthy orgasm. What seems most obvious about it, particularly when compared to the standards of mutual consent in love or marriage, is its radical individuality. It focuses on the single self, its needs and desires. The individual ought to do, by this criterion, that which enables him to get the sexual satisfaction he requires or enjoys. The philosopher might argue that this concern for self is rationally well justified. The only existence one truly knows or is aware of is one's own. We have no commensurate evidence for the reality of other persons as distinct from their bodies or their acts. Knowing only the reality of self, one should then be essentially concerned about what one does for himself. Ethical responsibility is most logically ego oriented. Since it has been abundantly well demonstrated that sexuality is a primary ingredient of human existence and that intercourse is its healthiest and most beneficial expression, the individual should seek to have healthy orgasms in accord with his personal needs. This may be a radically more liberal attitude toward sex relations than we have previously known, but it is precisely what reason calls for.

The psychologist might adduce other considerations which demand a new realism concerning the self. Man's primary drive is self-preservation, his most persistent motif in action, self-interest, the seeking of pleasure, and the avoiding of pain. Why do we want to hide from this basic reality of human existence and thereby create altruistic illusions about human conduct that can only lead to frustration and unhappiness? It would make for a far more honest and therefore less tense and troubled world if we took man for the self-concerned animal he is and built our ethical expectations around this.

I think it very important to accept the truth contained in this position. It must sound terribly harsh to those who take a romantic view of life, but the sooner they know that people are fundamentally selfish, the better it will be for them. When the chips are down, most people may be counted on to be more concerned for themselves than for others. To believe their friendliness goes deep, to accept their gestures of friendship or love as real and lasting is as easy as their later desertion is common and painful. This is also true socially. Corporations and politicians seek to project images of great personal concern. They are almost always more correctly assessed in terms of "what's in it for them"—generally profit or power. Such realism should not make us pessimistic or cynical, only more appreciative of personal love or social welfare become reality.

Of course, there are other people to whom we have some responsibility. What counts, however, is where the ethical emphasis is put. If everyone would look out for himself properly, we could have a much better, because more honest and less disillusioned, society. To put it more directly, while people should worry about others, if they do not act to fulfill their own sexual needs, no one will do so for them. More critically, if they do not take the initiative for a healthy sex life, they may rest assured our repressive society will keep them from one. In this area above all, the final loyalty must be to self.

This ethics, like every ethics, creates its own sense of responsibility. To be human enough to care about what one ought or ought not to do is by that act to submit oneself to obligations, even though they be self-determined. He who wishes to escape any sense of duty must never think but only plunge into choices. To be thoughtful and thus human is to be accountable, at the very least to oneself.

The ethics of healthy orgasm, therefore, creates its own sense of responsibility, in this instance limited to the acting individual himself. He should strive to have as much and as satisfying sex experience as he needs or enjoys. Because that is important to his existence, he should train and discipline himself to accomplish that good and even to sacrifice for it if necessary. Let me give two examples. First, he has the duty to guard against venereal disease, since the preservation of his life and health is basic to participation in sex. Despite antibiotic therapies there has been an incredible resurgence of venereal disease in recent years. In terms of the ethics of healthy orgasm, one must keep a sharp watch for any symptom of infection and immediately seek medical attention should he think he needs it. (I do not think the fear of contracting a venereal disease argues seriously against the possible rightness of any premarital intercourse. On the other hand, the common belief that "nice people" don't have such diseases is naive.)

When one is pursuing sexual activity to be true to oneself and one's needs, all intercourse which is not true to self is unjustified. The frequent use of orgasm as a means of losing one's identity, or the denial to oneself of sexual activity as a means of self-punishment for imagined guilt, is unethical. Similarly, one could not be true to oneself either through overindulgence or laziness in the pursuit of sexual activity.

The opponents of this point of view argue that it makes too much of sex and too little of other people. One gets the impression that orgasm is so central to human existence, that someone deprived of it can hardly be a person, that anyone whose life is not continually strengthened by intercourse cannot contribute creatively to society. That impression does not square with human experience or medical observation. There have been many people who have been kept from or who have renounced intercourse and yet have lived remarkably rich and useful lives. There seems to be no medical reason why one cannot do without orgasm for long stretches of time, even for life. Such absence may cause certain physiological tensions and may induce personal instability, narrowness of self, or in extreme cases mental illness. They need not. The sexual energies can find and often have found highly satisfactory outlets in forms other than orgasm. Not having intercourse is rarely the cause of mental pathology, though it may be the symptom of a serious psychic condition. Overt, genital sexual activity is important—that does not make it indispensable to being a whole person.

Conversely, to say that orgasm is beneficial does not make it therapeutic or the source of cultural productivity. Frequent sexual relations do not regularly prevent or cure mental illness. A high incidence of orgasms is no sign that one's paintings will be better or one's business more thoughtfully or energetically run.

This close identification of human health with vigorous intercourse is certainly not Freud's idea. Despite the truth of the criticism that he tended to look at man almost exclusively in a biological way, he still knew that man was far more than a creation of sexual intercourse. Freud saw personality as a far broader phenomenon than that which genital activity indicated. The libido—basic source of sexual energy—may be channeled most directly into intercourse, but not to see it as the fundamental life-seeking drive which properly flows out into all man's activities is not to understand it at all. Thus, to place so much emphasis on direct sexual fulfillment is to make too much of the sex act as such and to see too little of what it means to be a whole human being.

This difference in attitude and value emerges—perhaps in a somewhat unfair way—in the viewpoint of some sexual research. Kinsey and those who have followed his methods studied sexual behavior by counting people's orgasms. According to their hypothesis, to know when, where, and with whom orgasm occurred is to know something significant about human sexual activity. This procedure seems to reduce sexuality to the experience of orgasm and by its concentration on the quantitative aspects of the "outlets" confers equal value on each experience. Further, such research appears relatively unconcerned over the circumstances of the orgasm (e.g., masturbation, bestiality, with a prostitute or one's spouse). When man is reduced to his orgasmic activity, such an approach is likely. However, when his sexuality is seen as one part, though an important one, of his total being, the personal context of the orgasm will be as important as the orgasm itself.

A similar problem emerges on the interpretive level. Some people thought that the figures obtained by the researchers were normative. While Kinsey cannot be held to blame[76] for that illogical inference, he had hoped by gathering statistics to influence practice. One can understand concentration on the number of orgasms as a procedural necessity; how else can one quantify and thereby objectively study sexual activity? Yet in the unreflective mind, this easily becomes a standard or ideal. Significant sexual activity comes to mean having an orgasm, and the more orgasms one has, compulsives aside, the healthier one is. What began as an idea to make research more manageable is transformed into a standard of right and wrong. The opposing point of view must then be asserted: because empirical research cannot investigate man as he knows himself to be in his wholeness does not thereby justify saying he is only what numbers can grasp.

A further objection to the ethics of healthy orgasm is its extreme selfishness. It does not extend to others what it wants for self. More specifically, it does not make the concerns of the partner in intercourse as much a criterion of the act's rightness as those of the first party. The argument that one cannot prove the existence of others in the same way as one knows oneself to exist is not considered decisive. To the antagonists that says more about the problems of philosophy today than it does about the reality of other persons. We may not in any technical, philosophic sense "know" that other people are as real as we are and therefore probably entitled to be treated the way we wish to be treated. Still, this sense of mutual worth is quite common to all our important human contacts, and it has been basic to every major ethical idea (e.g., the Golden Rule, Kant's insistence on treating people as ends, or the democratic sense that all men are equal in dignity). Naturally the proponents of the love or marriage ethic, who value love as the highest expression of humanity, will consider the ethics of healthy orgasm an inferior, almost antihuman ethics.

The psychological data can be refuted in a similar way. People may behave largely in terms of concern for self. That is exactly why we consider them unethical or a-ethical much of the time. If they were thoughtful of others, their behavior would be far different and far better. Observation of their basic selfishness does not tell us what they should be or what they could be if they willed to change their perspective. The major problem with our society is not a paucity of orgasms but the encouragement of self-interest. We do not need more people living an orgasmic egoism but people who care about other people in the same way they care about themselves. Such human advances as have been made in history coincide precisely with this broadening of the moral horizon beyond self. When men stretched ethical duty from family to the clan, the tribe, the people, the nation as a whole, something wonderfully human was achieved. Our most important ethical task today is to learn to think of human duty in terms of all the men in this world. This does not imply altruistic self-surrender. On the contrary, as one can affirm one's particular selfhood, one finds the security for reaching out to another and accepting him as he is.

I agree with this stand against ethical egoism. I feel so strongly the harm it creates in sex (as in economics or politics), that I was strongly tempted not to include it as a form of sexual ethics at all. I did so because it is widely followed and because it can claim, under modern standards, to be a respectable intellectual structure for evaluating the desirability of sexual acts. It is an ethic in the technical sense of that term, i.e., a form of thoughtful guidance as to what one might responsibly do with one's freedom. However, I do not consider it ethical in the secondary meaning of that term, in granting to its standard a quality which is worthy of being called ethical. It makes individual autonomy absolute and then does not include the responsibility of respecting another's autonomy. I am committed to the dignity of persons other than myself. Moreover, I do not believe I can find worth and significance as a person unless I am as much involved with other people as myself. The imperative to be myself inevitably involves concern for other selves, for I am not fully separable from them. Hence, an ethic which does not involve them even as it involves me, is in my view no ethic. Intercourse takes place between two people. Not to have a fundamental concern for the other's will and freedom in evaluating the rightness of intercourse is an especially intimate breach of that need to consider others.

Something of this sense that right action must inevitably concern both parties is implicit in our language about sex. We have vulgar verbs for it, most of which society does not approve. We use them, conscious of their crudity and animality, often to show how visceral and glandular we are. All those terms are transitive verbs. They are what one person as subject does to another person as object. That is why they are properly underground words, for they express the selfishness of our sexuality before it has become moralized to a concern with others. I can understand that people who feel oppressed by the sexual inhibitions imposed by our society may want to use the gutter terms for intercourse from time to time to show their rebellion against the tyranny of society. But the reason for not employing these terms, even if one is uninhibited, is that they perpetuate a faulty morality. They express, perhaps foster, an egoistic attitude toward sex which considers other people the objects of one's acts. The immorality of obscenity is not in the words themselves but in their dehumanization of other people and thus, sooner or later, of us.

Because of the egoistic view of man implicit in the ethics of healthy orgasm, I cannot consider it a worthy possibility, as contrasted with the other three positions.

7

THE ETHICS OF MUTUAL CONSENT

THE STRENGTH OF the consent ethic lies in its insistence on the equal dignity of the parties considering having intercourse. It retains the high regard for sexuality of the healthy-orgasm view and considers sexual activity a primary good of man. It does not, however, make it so important to him that it overrides his obligation to be concerned for other people. It rather reverses those values. Here the intercourse is justified only when both parties freely agree to participate in it. In this way each individual's sexual needs are subordinated to the rights of the sexual partner to determine what he wishes to do. The one will have to overcome his sexual desires if the other does not freely wish to have intercourse. He must not in any way demand the consent he seeks merely because his sexual needs are great. Priority must be given to the other person's right to choose what to do. Not only is the self-centered quality of the ethics of healthy orgasm thereby overcome, but because the sexuality operates within the context of respect for others, it does not seem overexaggerated in its value to human existence.

Mutual consent may be called an ethical standard for sexual activity because two acknowledged human goods are placed in combination so that they reinforce each other. A person has regard for himself as well as the other by sharing freely in the pleasure of intercourse, while the act itself can be enjoyed on a more fully human level knowing one's partner is as willing to participate in it as oneself.

The choice is all that is required in this view, because sexual activity is primarily a private affair. They are benefiting one another while inflicting harm on no one. Were the acts done in public or as some sort of social outrage, were contraception not

being proficiently employed, others might well be concerned.
Yet, as long as care is taken to preserve the private nature of
the sexual act, all that is needed to validate it between the partners is their freely given consent. Therefore, too, as long as minors, neurotics, and others who cannot really be expected to
give honest consent are not concerned, and as long as there is no
seduction, subtle barter, or any other form of coercion taking
place, this must be called an ethical view.

This criterion claims the great merit of freeing us from an unreasonable repression of our sexuality while limiting it by an
ethical concern for other persons and their needs. Is this
not the major acceptable truth of the sexual revolution of
our time, that we have been sexually restrained beyond any
meaningful justification and that any sexual morality which
would speak to modern man must begin with his need for
greater freedom? That desire for a more natural style of existence, one which would understand wholesomeness in terms of
the body as well as the spirit, is what powers the call for a new
sex ethics. Modern contraception and the cures for venereal disease are enabling factors. By virtually eliminating the potential
adverse effects of sexual intercourse, they make possible a new
liberality toward it. The studies of the sexual practices of
recent generations are interpreted as saying that the ethics of
marriage is far too restrictive for most people. It is simply unreasonable physiologically. In our society everyone marries
many years after puberty. If they are pursuing long-range educational or business goals, a decade or more of their most
sexually significant years passes before marriage and the legitimation of intercourse. What is suffered in waiting for the right
mate or, worse, grabbing for one so as to have one is well known.
No wonder that ethic never worked even when pregnancy was a
great risk. No wonder the Jewish community called for teen-age
marriages, arranged by parents, to channel sexuality. With
college and, increasingly, graduate school ahead, marriages in
high school or at high school graduation hardly seem a realistic
possibility for many people in our society. For them to postpone
marriage would by the old standards mean to postpone inter-

course. While ethics must channel biology and structure social forms, it cannot seem reasonable or effective if it seeks radically to deny the body or the demands of the culture. Asking sexually mature adolescents to postpone intercourse for four or five years is a denial of fundamental needs. Insisting that they restrain themselves for eight or ten or twelve years may be destructive.

By the same token the love criterion is also too restrictive, if we take it seriously and are unwilling to view it as a variety of mutual consent, though scented with the perfumes of romance. Genuine love is rare, though certainly more common than genuine marriage. Since our discussion centers on the painful years before marriage, love must surely mean that occasional spark that for a time joyously illuminates the years of maturation. Obviously, intercourse is appropriate to lovers, for theirs is a special case of mutual consent founded on a close personal relationship. They can bring a depth of emotion and personal exchange to their sexual relations which will surely enrich and ennoble them. Yet love is an unusual situation. To limit sexual relations to it is to suggest a standard that is needlessly repressive. Most sexually mature people are not in love throughout the years preceding their marriage. Our great appreciation of love must not blind us to the naturalness and desirability of sexual activity. When people are not in love, they are still sexual beings, needing sexual expression to be more fully healthy, wholesome persons.

By contrast, making the mutual consent of two reasonably mature people the criterion of the rightness of sexual intercourse results in great sexual freedom, but within ethical limits. Assent is much easier to find than love, but insisting that it come from a person who is stable enough to understand and assume the responsibility for the decision does not make it cheap or common. Many people, for their own reasons, will be moved to say "No" under certain circumstances. The need to respect the other person's right to choose freely, even should that choice be "No," is a great moral responsibility. It is one thing to say "you are free to make up your own mind no matter what the decision" and another to mean it when the decision is negative. We all resent a rebuff; hence, consciously or unconsciously we bring pressure to bear on someone from whom a rebuff might be forthcoming. Egoism is basic to life, and therefore an honest concern for mutuality in a relationship is an important ethical consideration and an enviable human accomplishment. So partisans of the criterion of mutual consent believe they have given the best possible balance to man's need for sexual activity and his ethical obligations to others.

The critical values involved in the question of premarital intercourse are now before us. Each of the three remaining options—consent, love, marriage—agrees that it should take place only when both parties come to it by free decision. They disagree on whether that is the only consideration for judging the act ethical. Is it enough that the couple comes to it of their own volition? Or is that free choice itself only appropriate when a certain quality of personal relations exists between them? At one end of the spectrum is the proposition that sex is good and consent is all that is needed to validate it. At the other end, there is concern with what constitutes a proper reason for saying "Yes," and that is interpreted in terms of what the persons mean to one another. Though sex is good, it should ethically be consented to only when one loves or is married to the other person. Mature decision alone no longer justifies the sex, but only the *quality of feeling* toward the other which makes this particular use of one's freedom responsible.

Since all three views affirm that sex is good and freedom is necessary, the difference between them concerns the relative value attached to what the partners mean to one another. For the ethics of mutual consent, the human involvement of one person with another may be a highly desirable thing, but it would rank the need for sexual expression higher. The consenting parties need not know each other long or well, nor need they be greatly attached to one another. Let them meet and freely agree in their maturity to have intercourse, and there is no good reason why they should not do so. Indeed, because sexuality is important to man and therefore beneficial to society, there is good reason why they should.

The protagonists of the ethics of love as well as those of marriage reverse the ranking. For them the sexual activity, though important, is secondary to what the persons mean to one another. Only when they are deeply devoted to one another—or, in the other view, when they are so devoted to one another that they are pledged to one another formally—is their intercourse right. Their criticism of the ethics of mutual consent is based on this different ranking of the values.

If the genius of intercourse by consent is that it makes sex far freer, the complaint is that it makes it too free. One need not hold a negative attitude toward sex to argue that there is a substantial difference between affirming sexuality and encouraging sexual intercourse. It is one thing to say that man's basic energies are sexual and need healthy and continual expression. It is quite another to assert that only a continual series of coital orgasms can accomplish this. If greater health and personal well-being are the goal of a newer set of sexual standards, then these must be gained by first creating proper attitudes toward sex, beginning with the recognition that there are many forms, other than genital, of expressing one's sexuality. The process would continue by providing many opportunities for friendly heterosexual activities, social outlets for the creative energies, and from the viewpoint of the love ethic, by agreeing that those in love may legitimately have intercourse if they wish to.

There seems, in the argument for the ethics of mutual consent, to be too easy an identification of person with sex and sex with intercourse. Being a person seems so dependent on sexual intercourse that, except for concern with one's freedom to choose, the self is entirely subordinated to the need for intercourse. The opposite can much more cogently be argued, say the antagonists. Who a person is determines the meaning of his sexual acts, and not vice versa.[77] There are many people who are impotent or frigid because they are unable to accept their sexuality on a more intimate personal level. Their cure must take place in the dynamics of the self, and only then are they capable of normal sexual activity. If they are ruled out of consideration because their psychological handicap is a certain immaturity, consider the normal case of intercourse by consent alone. The person's interest is in orgasm with an accepting and acceptable partner. Will it be on the same level as intercourse which proceeds out of a genuine regard and concern for the other? Though the consent means there is, strictly speaking, no exploitation of the one by the other, what it practically amounts to is an agreement for mutual exploitation. Each needs a sexual partner and is therefore only concerned that the other give consent and then satisfaction. The real interest in the other is as an instrument for increasing one's sexual pleasure.

The foregoing is not just a theoretical analysis but the reality behind every pick-up. Most people are not so inhuman as simply to announce what they are looking for and then do it with whoever is immediately willing and acceptable. They want a certain personal preplay, some exchange of pleasant talk and light companionship which will give a personal quality to the sex act. Yet, in fact, all this standard calls for is mutual consent, not any special level of human involvement. It is the sexual use, one of the other, masked by the initial exchanges. To relate to other people in this reductive sexual way is to abet that brutalizing cultural style in which persons are treated in terms of their roles or functions, rather than as whole persons. If there is any place in our lives where we should try to be ourselves and treat others in full human depth, it is in our sexual relations. This is a most intimate act, arousing the most sensitive human feelings in an extraordinary harmony of body and spirit. If this act now can be seen essentially as two people giving each other a needed outlet or pleasure, can there be any hope that society will learn in more external matters to care about persons in their fullness?

That argument is convincing enough for some people to modify the terms of the consent ethics to say that the partners should at least have a genuine regard for one another. The character of the association, its very preciousness, and not just its basis in free choice, should justify what happens between the parties involved. They should be friends and not just acquaintances. This recognizes the fundamental problem, that freedom, while necessary for an ethical response, cannot be the only consideration involved in sexual decision. The objection from the love or marriage view is that sex is still too much and the interpersonal, too little. In the first place, the friendship criterion is too vague to be meaningful. One can well imagine what would happen to this standard under the pressure of sex drives or interests. We are already so depersonalized that in desperation many people need only a beer or two to make believe they are really your friend. If friendship means a genuine concern for the person as person and not just as sexual channel, then such friendships are rare.

Second, now that a shift in values from the strictly sexual to the personal has been made, has the balance between the factors been properly determined? What makes real friendship different from mere acquaintance is already the quality of affection. It is the intimations of love in the friendship—the trust, the concern, the willingness to give—that make it possible to think of friendship as a possible standard for rightness of intercourse. Yet shouldn't that make love or marriage the only proper context for an act as significant as intercourse? Intercourse hardly seems meant to be a common occurrence. Physically it is somewhat intricate, its performance requiring a certain skill by both partners to give great satisfaction. It conveys a supreme emotional experience, but that, like all other joys, is easily lost with too frequent or too deliberate participation. Above all, it has a unique potentiality, for it might create a life. All these qualities should put it on a level other than holding hands, kissing, or petting. On the human level, then, intercourse is too important not to be reserved for those with whom one shares the ultimate in personal relationships. Friendship deserves its intimacies—sharing, giving, and the more ordinary forms of sexual exchange, like companionship, dancing, or kissing. It does not merit the greatest intimacy of them all, the sharing of the most extraordinary act of which persons are regularly capable. That makes sense only when the lovers share the greatest personal intimacy—love. In that situation the deed is appropriate to the personal reality. Sex follows self and is fully interpreted in terms of it. In love, the intercourse is not merely an exercise in reduction of the sex drive or a pursuit of pleasure but both of them transformed by the special quality of the partners' more embracing relationship with one another.

There is also a negative factor to be considered. If intercourse is engaged in with persons one does not love, it cannot retain the unique meaning it might have when shared by lovers. Thus, as the love advocates see it, previous intercourse with other partners is not disturbing when one knows it had been done only out of love. The intercourse remains precious, even though not exclusive, for it remains the rare expression for the rare relationship. But the more freely intercourse had been engaged in previously, the less would its personal meaning necessarily be when finally it is claimed to be offered in love.

One additional matter must be raised here against the consent theory on behalf of the advocates of marriage. If premarital intercourse were validated by mutual consent, even on the basis of friendship, what would the effects on the institution of marriage be? Let us assume, for example, that many people in their youth had sexual intercourse with anyone who was reasonably congenial and friendly with them. Later, when they want to have a family, they marry. The problem in their intercourse now is greater than their knowing that this act means nothing very special to their relationship, for they have participated in it as part of diverse relationships. The new difficulty is why they should not continue the old practice even though they are now married.[78] If it was ethical then, why is it not ethical now? The wedding ceremony will not prevent them from making friends with or being attracted sexually to other people. If satisfying intercourse is important to being a healthy person and one's secretary or neighbor's husband promises refreshed experience, wouldn't such extramarital relations be desirable? As long as they are willing and reasonably friendly, wouldn't it be wrong to deny oneself and, logically, one's mate such activity? The force of that argument appeals to many married people today. One reads occasionally of couples granting each other sexual freedom, the mutual-consent theory now reinterpreting the marriage pledges. There are couples who trade partners and groups with various devices for intermixing the participants. They are the sensationalistic fringe realities of a society where adultery may be sad but hardly uncommon, where some people use frequent divorce as a substitute for infidelity. Can the institution of marriage, based as it has been on the faithfulness of the partners to one another, long survive a standard which not only permits but encourages extramarital intercourse? And if the stable family is weakened, what will happen to the fabric of our society?

In the traditional marriage the exclusiveness of the sex relations is the major, continuing sign of the unique personal relation of husband and wife to each other. Should their intercourse be shared with others, even though having a family is reserved to the marriage partner, what they mean to one another could not be the same. As their exclusivity disappears, as the circle of their most intense intimacy expands, they change radically the kind of marital union which enfolds them. Adultery is not just a transgression of an old law and a personal promise but a change in the relationship one has with his spouse. Sexual fidelity bespeaks ultimate personal faithfulness, exclusive regard, unique concern. Adultery therefore is never trivial and though we may forgive, if we love, we cannot cease caring.

Thus, the objection is that the ethics of mutual consent weakens the hope of stable marriages and secure families. That has a *social* as well as a personal significance.[79] No single human institution seems to have as great an effect on the formation of high moral character as the loving home. Wherever society finds its humanizing concerns balked, there, almost always, broken and unstable family units will be the cause. Every social problem—the school dropouts, emotional disturbance, delinquency, violent crime—seems rooted in poor family ties. Yet our culture does not take marriage seriously enough. Many people treat it casually. If this one does not work out, they can always divorce and try again. If a spouse makes more demands than he provides comfort or pleasure, perhaps one should look for a better match.

The divorce rate is high; commitment to marital responsibility is low. That is a serious social problem. It should not be amplified by choosing, when one is young, a sexual standard that will later be an obstacle in the way of establishing a healthy family based on a strong marriage. Sexual faithfulness is the best way a married couple can bring to one another a continuing sense of the unique importance of their relationship. Therefore, it is a major hope in their effort to defend their marriage against the destructive forces our society will deploy against it.

The Jews have almost certainly managed to foster personal morality and social concern despite immersion in many brutal cultures because they have given such high religious significance to marriage and the family. Their homes were founded on the sexual faithfulness of husband and wife, and the overwhelming majority of Jews through the ages found that standard not only practical but humanly fulfilling. Even in the *pilegesh* relationship of the Middle Ages, the woman was less a mistress than almost a wife.[80] She was not a stray prostitute or a friend, but someone taken into one's house, "set aside for oneself," "married." The formality and binding quality of marriage were missing, but the relationship had relative permanence and a socially sanctioned structure. If that was the only pattern of nonmarital sexual relations ever legally recognized in Judaism, one can see how dear to it were marriage and fidelity.

A word must also be said from the marriage view about what it means to become a full person. The child and society are not alone in needing a strong family. Marriage, not friendship or love, is where most individuals work out and win their maturity. Business, communal, or social success can readily be achieved with the involvement of only parts of one's personality. There, in fact, achievement can often come only when one suppresses his ethics or taste or compassion. In the close personal association of a family the whole self is most fully at stake. There one is seen regularly, unguardedly, in every mood and in an extraordinary variety of circumstances. One can perhaps dominate an industry by one's power, or sway an organization by one's image. In a family, technical competence will take one only so far. In the process of responding to the personal demands of mate and the changing realities of children, the real self emerges. The family may end up playing a game of illusion with one of its members because they know him for what he is really, but loving or respecting him, they agree to treat him as what he would like to be. But we are speaking not of those who must live a lie but who still want to be persons in the face of reality. They will not find it more fully and more demandingly than by marrying and raising a family. That is why in Judaism both are considered religious duties, commands of God. To this day, thanks to generations of communal practice and despite contemporary disbelief, the Jewish community knows that marriage is about the most important thing that happens in a person's life. Many Jewish parents still scrutinize every date as if a proposal were imminent, and Jewish adults consider anyone who is unmarried in need of their matchmaking expertise.

Obviously the objections to the standard of mutual consent by the love and marriage protagonists stem from a different ranking of the values involved. All the alternative views agree sex, self, and society merit our concern and guide our action. They differ first on whether sexual activity is to be subordinated to what it means to be a person, as in the love criterion, or, further, whether the quality of the interpersonal relations must be such as to require formal structure, namely, marriage.

The mutual-consent position is by no means refuted by these vigorous attacks. There is much it can say in response. One tack would be to argue that maybe it is time to change the institution of marriage. The monogamous marriage of equal partners is not that old, and considering the amount of adultery and the many mistress relationships it has engendered—with the Jewish community no exception—maybe it is time to take another step forward. One might well argue that a good deal of the difficulty with contemporary marriage is that its sexual standard is too rigid. Affluence, leisure, mobility, and effective contraception have made practical a marital style that was formerly necessarily suppressed. As polygamy and concubinage eventually gave way to a supposedly strict monogamy, so the social changes in recent years make possible a marriage which countenances sex for pleasure while restricting it in relation to having and raising children. This plan of marital sexuality would be more in keeping with biological and social realities and could therefore be more effectively practiced. It would, as a result, bring to marital relations today a greater stability, a different sort of quality than they now know.

The strongest rejoinder, however, is a defense of the primacy of sexuality by an attack on the repressiveness of the other views. What are young people expected to do until love or marriage, tire their libido with physical exercise or swim away their sexual urges? Dating is hardly a satisfactory substitute for intercourse. It is more likely to be an inducement. And sexual contact short of intercourse is neither satisfactory nor without its own damage. Would the advocates of the love or marriage standards say masturbation is more ethical than intercourse by mutual consent? Would they consider heavy petting leading to orgasm more virtuous than the willing intercourse of two mature persons? Surely there is something perverse in favoring a technical virginity which permits everything but intercourse yet stops short of allowing the culminating satisfaction.[81] One thereby allows almost all of its intimacy but few of its benefits for the sake of preserving a normal act for unusual situations. Only those who have not experienced or who have forgotten the burning sexual needs of youth could be so blind to the anguish the honest application of their criterion of intercourse would engender.

These arguments, and others which might be offered, bite. The difficulty in making a choice now begins to be evident. It continues to deepen as we examine the arguments pro and con for using love as our criterion.

8

THE ETHICS OF LOVE

LOVE SEEMS a miracle because the lovers have such overwhelming concern for each other and accept each other fully for what they are. One can easily be intrigued by one person's smile or excited by the way another person talks, but one loves his darling entire. That will include what previously or even now in the midst of love one finds annoying. Still these are insignificant concerns compared to the richness of the love, so one gladly learns to live with them. On the contrary, all the quirks and idiosyncrasies of the beloved are now seen in terms of his full personal depth, and he, for all that, is loved. For anyone to be accepted and affirmed in this way is as precious as it is rare.

Our beloved is so concerned with our welfare, he will struggle to provide us with whatever we need or desire. He will do anything to prevent harm from befalling us. More, he cares not only for what we are but for what we yet will be. He recognizes our potential and helps us try to reach it. Love thus validates our existence as nothing else can and, with an unparalleled immediacy, helps turn us into the people we knew we always were meant to be.

So love always involves a sense of the unique and the exclusive. One feels he has found that single, special person in all the world meant for him. That beloved and no other brings unparalleled delight, incomparable inner joy. To like someone is quite different. Then others are or might be equally interesting. Their affection has little sense of irreplaceable depth, of fundamental personal affirmation. When a delightful companion goes, we are sad. When true love goes, we say, quite seriously, it has "died." An experience as precious as life itself is now over. Some day another love may come along, but we know it will be different, as unique in its own way and worth as this one was.

Love does all that for us. If it does not, if it has somehow not made us more truly ourselves, then it is very likely not love. Love, by definition then, fulfills and exalts. Sexual intercourse in such a context cannot be wrong. When two people affirm each other in their fullness, to include sexual expression as one more facet of their sharing together is logical and indeed most appropriate. The act is not only validated by the relationship, but because full personal acceptance is primary, the biological sexuality of the partners is now transformed from the merely animal to the uniquely human. What more fitting setting could there be for the unique interpersonal act of intercourse than the unique, full-scale, interpersonal affirmation called love?

The mutual-consent protagonist will find this insistence on the unique quality of love a laughable romanticism. He might in hard-boiled realism insist people can and do love several others at the same time. Much of that depends on one's emotional energy, for love should really be understood as a sense of heightened feeling or a temporary fixation of interest. There are those fascinating situations described in literature in which one person loved two others equally, sometimes leading to a *ménage à trois*. Besides, many people never get to love someone in any qualitatively unique way.

Yet these criticisms do not disturb the advocates of the ethics of love. They point out that its sense of the singular has been widely enough known in time and across cultures that it must be considered a fundamental capacity of man, and one widely fulfilled at that. True, it does not happen to everyone and is often confused with romantic fantasies. That does not make it less real or desirable. If people could acknowledge how important love is to them, they might work harder to overcome the sensuality and selfishness which keep them from finding love. They might then insist that society, instead of commercializing love, should provide better means by which people could truly get to know one another.

Our society does not encourage honest love and create the

social patterns which would foster it. Rather, it exploits love by reducing it to sexual terms and then subjects us to a continuous campaign of sexual stimulation and arousal. Writers vie to see who can sell better by arousing more, and photographers are engaged in a contest to see who can show the most provocative pictures and not be censored. The mass media make one feel inadequate because one is not alive enough sexually and then regardless of one's experience one is made to feel even more inadequate in terms of the images of orgasmic virtuosity constantly held up for imitation. We are exploited through our sexuality and robbed of our ability to love wholly and humanly. In such a pandering culture there is appropriateness in the call for a freer standard of sexual relations. That does not mean we need an extension of the current anti-Puritan spree but rather a situation in which love can flower normally. The consent ethic could be satisfied with our current social style as long as its tacit approval of free sex were made open and accepted. The love ethic knows this society is sick because antipersonal. It is therefore far more radical and revolutionary.

Real love would by this standard justify intercourse, but it does not necessarily enjoin it. The lovers may decide for reasons of their own that they do not wish to have intercourse, that they are satisfied with less physically intense or personally involving expressions of their feelings for one another. This is, of course, their right. Love entitles them to it. It does not rob them of their freedom, for the ethics of love must include the ethics of mutual consent or it is neither ethical nor loving.

In this connection it is interesting to note the different effect the love ethic tends to have on men and women, as reported by some researchers. When love is real, the men report more compunction about the rightness of intercourse, even though they may approve of and have had intercourse with girls they did not love. For girls the opposite seems to be true. Where they would normally object to intercourse before marriage, if they really love a man, they are far more willing than he to consider it proper. If he loves her, he is inclined to wait until he has married her. That is his form of concern for her. If she loves him, she is inclined to sleep with him now. That is her way of responding to their relationship. If this gives a reasonably accurate description of the actual operation of this criterion, then, though it is more liberal than the marriage standard, its general adoption would not necessarily result in a much freer practice than now actually obtains. Paradoxically it might, by insisting on deep personal involvement, be more restrictive.

The love criterion is held superior to the one requiring marriage because it claims that the relationship, not any formality connected with it, is crucial. Both affirm the value of love. The issue between them would rather seem to be one of time, so to speak. Why should only a lifelong relationship be considered sufficiently significant to justify intercourse? That may once have been necessary, because sexual relations always meant the likelihood of children. It was the reason Nachmanides gave, against Maimonides, when he said that the prohibition of nonmarital intercourse in Judaism rests only on Rabbi Eleazar's reasoning that, if people had intercourse indiscriminately, children of unknown parentage would abound and incest would soon be common. If proficient contraception is assumed, then that traditional reason for intercourse only in lifelong relationships no longer holds. Now the meaning of the persons to one another, not any ceremony or license, can and should be the basis of judging whether intercourse is right.

In large part, society has already accepted that shift of values in its conception of marriage. It is not so long ago that personal love was subordinated to the roles the husband and wife assumed in the marital state. They did not marry out of personal concern but because people were supposed to. They did not think of marital happiness in terms of individual fulfillment and growth of self. Though Judaism recognized rights of refusal in matchmaking and the possibility of subsequent divorce, the couple's love was normally expected to arise as a by-product of their being married and living together. Today's marriage has another tone. There are still role expectations to structure the relationship, and when each partner has the psychic strength to fulfill them, they often are the basis for a deepening of the love the couple has for each other. Nonetheless, people hope to marry because they have found someone they genuinely care for, and they hope to stay together because of what they continue to mean to one another personally. Most people consider that new marital idea a moral advance, since it provides a greater opportunity for each person to be more truly himself. The difference is illuminated by our attitude when the marriage has come to a crisis. In the older system people tended to stay married regardless of personal fulfillment because marriage was a social necessity. Today when a couple finds living together inhibits the best in them and damages their lives, almost everyone can understand why they must divorce. And should they no longer really love one another but decide in mutual respect to continue living together for the sake of the children, we may accept that as a reasonable decision, but we will not be happy about such a marriage. Personal fulfillment in the relationship is our new and better ideal.

The recent shift from social to personal criteria in our judgment makes a successful marriage quite difficult to achieve. We are more demanding of the partners than in previous generations. They must not merely play the father or mother role properly but must validate the role by their personal authenticity and find a way to remain just that real in all that befalls them as the years go by. That is why we have so many poor marriages today. Many of us are not mature or resourceful enough to live that sort of life and help others achieve it. Still, having seen marriages where time has continually enriched each of the persons and their relationship, we cannot go back to an older, comparatively impersonal pattern.

If that is true even of our view of marriage, then the love itself, not the performance of some rites, is what identifies the most significant human relationship. This means love should be the sole criterion of the rightness of sexual intercourse in marriage, as it was before it. Unloving intercourse in marriage, though socially countenanced, is unethical, whereas loving intercourse outside of marriage, though society still claims to disapprove of it, is right and proper.

This ethic, too, imposes certain obligations on those who affirm it. Of careful contraception and precautions against venereal disease, enough has been said. The special duties here derive from the use of love as our criterion.

The first thing to be said is that both partners should make reasonably certain they are in love. This is not a simple matter, since one cannot give any precise definition of love or indicate how it may be recognized or its counterfeits avoided. Anyone who has been in love will tell you that it is glorious and that you will know it when it happens (by the same sort of reasoning which is applied to knowing there is a God). It will often be added that it is easy to be fooled. This being the case, to be true to the criterion means that the doubt or uncertainty of either lover is sufficient reason for them not to have intercourse. Only love justifies intercourse; any question about its actual presence nullifies it.

This suggestion, that hesitation is a good safeguard against infatuation or simple sexual desire, should be extended. Love's arrival is generally not swift. It grows and flowers in time. Hence, any sudden progression from dating to loving to bed should be looked upon with great suspicion. Real love should show more personal concern than ever to rush. It more likely would make the question of having intercourse a matter of the most thoughtful consideration. It would want to avoid exploiting the other person in any possible way. The relationship ought to have lasted for quite a while to qualify as love rich enough to make intercourse right. Time certainly proves little, but if it is weeks rather than months, it is more likely to be friendship enriched with passion than a genuine love. A little patience to see what it turns out to be should not destroy, though it may test, love. A good sign of love is the understanding one gives the other when their views diverge, particularly on something so important and so personal as sexual relations. Thus, the response to "If you really loved me, you'd have intercourse with me" is probably "If you really loved me, you'd stop pressuring me." The love criterion is truly far more restrictive than that which only demands consent, but this is precisely because it demands the whole person and not just his will.

It is also revealing to note the frequency with which one is in love. Some people are continually falling in and out of love. Initially, there is something quite charming about the idea. On repetition it seems immature and foolish. Love which continually comes and goes is likely not to be love. The person who is in love for the fourth time in one semester had better take a good look at himself. And if in every case it is connected with the proposal that the lovers sleep together, then the heart is obviously not the primary source of stimulation.

In contrast to this, many a man is willing to settle down in a relationship he calls love, but more realistically he wants a housekeeper, and one attractive enough to take care of his sexual needs as well. For a woman, living with someone is a good form of social security. It ends the dating problem and the loneliness of not dating. Both are appealing. Neither is love.

Nor can love be understood as a justification of habitual intercourse. Today's feelings give us no right to go to bed together next week. Love sanctions intercourse when love is present. When it is not present, then regardless of what we have meant to each other, no intercourse is now permitted. We are not speaking here of the obvious situation, that is, when love is over, the sexual practices terminate. This is self-evident, though most people find it difficult to admit to one another that their love has ended. The subtler point is that during the affair itself, there are moments, sometimes long periods, when love wanes. What was rich and moving is now only nice, perhaps even dull. We generally tend to deny the reality of such moments because we exult in the heights of mutual understanding we have reached together. When our love is new and deliciously surprising, we cannot believe, we refuse to believe, that there will be hours when things become almost as they were before we began to love. When our love matures, we know it cannot always be ecstasy. We still have a right to say that we are in love, for we trust that the special experience will soon return. If it does not, we shall be in torment. If it remains missing, we must break off with our old sweetheart. But that faith in the return of the immediacy of love is often rewarded. Love returns, usually renewed and invigorated. Man being finite, such times of emptiness will occur even in the deepest love, and they will be succeeded by a return of the love. (Again, love is the best analogy to faith in God.)

The point in acknowledging this cycle of the reality of the sense of love is that only the presence of love validates intercourse. Trust in the relationship or its return does not. For lovers to make intercourse a habit, a meaningless routine, is unethical by the love criterion. Love is anything but mechanical or automatic. It will, despite sexual urges, respect the partner's right to say no to it.

I do not see that this loyalty to one's real feelings in each specific situation detracts from what was said previously about preparedness for contraception. One might argue that having mechanical means at hand, or regularly taking pills, was already a commitment to the deed. However, there is a practical as well as a logical difference between being prepared "in case" and having decided in fact. Possession does not require utilization, but nonpossession must, though love suggests it, ethically nullify the intercourse. Obviously, making provision for contraception indicates that the person might consider having intercourse. Many people simply do not wish to be that conscious of, and therefore that responsible for, what they may later do. They would rather risk pregnancy than face the fact that they may want to have intercourse. So if there is a chance the lovers may have intercourse, even though it seems unlikely at the moment, they should remember that moods change and therefore that they should be ready with contraception even though they never use it. This is not a concession to habit but an admission that intercourse is still possible between them—but only on condition no child will be conceived.

The love ethic is a serious and demanding one. It is neither libertine nor easy to obey. Since its standard is so personal, the full burden of decision must be borne by the individuals involved themselves, and they must determine anew in each situation what they believe it is right for them to do.

There are, of course, objections to this proposal. We have

already heard those from the vantage point of the mutual-consent theory. Now we must hear criticism from the advocates of the marriage criterion. Before that, however, an exposition of the marital standard itself is called for.

9

THE ETHICS OF MARRIAGE

To THOSE WHO uphold the marriage criterion, love is a necessary condition for intercourse but not a sufficient one. What is needed to make it satisfactory is a sense of what kind of love this must be, for there are different levels of love. As friendship is almost but not quite love, so ordinary love is wonderful but not yet the level of personal fulfillment which brings two people to pledge their whole lives to one another. This is the ultimate in human relationships, and this is why it is argued that sexual intercourse, the ultimate in regular interpersonal acts, is right only in the context of marriage.

This view sees formal marriage as the appropriate state for two people whose love goes so deep, they know they must live out the rest of their lives with one another. Their judgment may later turn out to be wrong, and a divorce may be desirable, a reality Judaism has always acknowledged. Still they know they mean so much to one another, they cannot only think in terms of the present. Each feels the meaning of his life so fully bound up with his love, that he cannot dissociate himself as he will be from the loved one who glorifies his present. Thus, he wants his love to be part of his future for all the time granted him. When that is how they both feel, they marry to signify that level of devotion and to pledge to one another their willingness to undertake the serious responsibilities of this interdependent way of living.

This explains love only in terms of them, but their communion is most fully realized in begetting children. The tragedy of infertility is that the ultimate blending of the two persons in one is now frustrated. In mingling the very genetic stuff of which they are made they unite most intimately and project their love into time to be. Now their love is oriented not merely to their own lifetime, but it is extended through their children's lifetime as well. This kind of love, the sort that is determined to create and foster new life, solemnizes its existence and acknowledges its special duties in marriage rites and vows.

If the two people know what they mean to one another, why do they need pledges, publicly made and solemnly attested? Why is it not enough for them to live together in love? They might well do so, and that is why most state laws and, in some special circumstances, the Jewish religion both recognize the validity of common-law marriage. Yet even here, the reality of the relationship of two people is judged not just by its mood or tone, but by the acts they did, by how long they lived together, and by the ways in which they showed their concern for one another. Longevity and devotion have been substituted for the wedding rites. They proved what the relationship was. Had nothing been said between them and had it not been confirmed by what in fact took place, there would have been no significant relationship. The words and deeds did not create what there was between them, but without some statement whose reality was attested to in life, they would not know what they truly meant to each other and thus would not have had their love. Something must be done to indicate the truth between them, particularly if the relationship lasts over years. The only questions, then, in any serious love are, What words? or What acts?

No ceremony can create or maintain love between a couple. No rites can guarantee that those now entitled to call themselves husband and wife will live together in the sort of developing, personal mutuality that modern men hope for. To that extent, all marriages are better judged after many years than when the bride and groom come down the aisle. This existential truth tells us little about how people ought to begin such a life-to-life relationship. When two people are ready to acknowledge that their lives now take on meaning primarily from one another, it is too important a matter to be passed by or slipped into. It is too great a human decision and accomplishment not to be celebrated. It is too direct an entry into the age-old process of biologic continuity not to be ritualized and symbolized. The words are a mockery if love is not there. Yet, though the highest love be present, the words are not unnecessary. In saying them, what was only felt and formless becomes definite and specific. Having said them is itself an act which, by raising emotion to conscious deed, changes the relationship by making it fully self-conscious and socially public. It is like the difference between knowing you love one another and finally having the courage to put it into words. When commitment can be recognized in action, one can have more trust that it is real, though no insurance. The wedding pledges unite the couple in a way that no reliance on mood ever can.

Part of the effectiveness of these vows is that they are made in public. Knowing we must make our pledges before others makes us less likely to lie to our beloved or ourselves. Privately, in one another's embrace, it is easy to say we love and that our love justifies our giving ourselves to one another. The oldest gambit of the seduction game is to plead one's love and then quickly proceed to its demands.[82] Such intimate declarations often take on a different light after orgasm or when a pregnancy is discovered. Yet when we know our mutual promises will only be taken seriously if we make them so all men may know whom we have chosen and what we have pledged, we are apt to promise ourselves far less rashly and to stand behind what we said we would do.

Besides, society has a stake in this new relationship. We might prefer to think of ourselves as purely private persons and our decision to link our lives with another as our affair alone. That is largely but not entirely true. Our families brought us into being and nurtured us to independence, hoping we would one day reach the fulfillment of love that leads to marriage. When we come to that moment so vital to our existence, our families have a stake in its proper celebration. To deny it to them is to reject the link between the generations in the name of the independence of self. True, they do not own us, but they gave us biological existence and confirmed it in their love. If we insist we have no obligations to them, how will it ever be possible for us to acknowledge the responsibilities love brings to every spouse and parent?

Society, too, has been concerned to bring us to this day, although this fact is more difficult to acknowledge with appreciation, since society's morality is so flawed and its failures so great a burden on us. Nonetheless, the moral values it has sought to create, albeit imperfectly, are, as it knows, founded upon stable, strong marriages. It is concerned with our marriage for what it means to us as persons and for what our marriage can mean to building a better society. It hopes, by requiring registration and other such formalities, to help the persons involved realize theirs is a social as well as a private state, one with duties to community as well as to self. Among Jews, every marriage is a clan affair, for this folk has long believed that most people become full persons only in marriage and that the Jewish people itself can only perpetuate its stubborn service to God by families reflecting that purpose.

Particularly since marriage implies having and raising children, the stake of family and society in the marital relationship should be clear. To deny it would imply that we can be ourselves without reference to other men, that we owe nothing to the people whose food we have eaten, whose protection we enjoy, whose culture has made us the sort of individual we are. We may want to protest against or reject one or another aspects of our society —and not to do so but to become a silent partner to its stupidities is already to be immoral—but to deny society's involvement in a marriage is to misunderstand our continuing need for a real community in which alone we can find the context to be a properly private self.

Marriage involves us in all that and more. Hence, if it is not based on the fullest depth of concern, it cannot be what it ought to be. No wonder that its pledges need to be as solemn as men are capable of—before an officer of the court for secular marriage; before God for religious marriage. Entering it in terms of the most significant values one knows is still no guarantee of success but is the most realistic way for one who hopes to create his most significant human relationship.

One of the reasons—and one rarely discussed—why marriage is so difficult today is that many people do not know what it means to care about something with all one's heart and soul and might. Accordingly, they do not know how to bring the proper depth of concern and dedication to marriage. For them, taking a spouse turns out to be an unexpected discovery of what it means to care for others or for whatever else in fact they really do care about. To have to wait that long to get to know themselves is, too often, a tragic delay. They discover they are too immature for marriage, for they have not learned how to care consistently or enough. Or they or their spouse may now care differently about things than they had previously thought. If what they each want to give and get from life is deeply divergent, then how can they live together in ultimate sharing? So it is desperately important for people to try to know what they really stand for before they are married, at least insofar as they can. The marriage vows are spoken in terms of ultimate values, as a guide and hopefully in the reality that only when marriage is entered on that level can it truly be called marriage.

This analysis has gone on at such length because in the debate between the advocates of the love and the marriage criteria the former insist that marriage adds nothing to what love brings or creates. Now we can see that two matters divide them. One is the extent of the individual's involvement with society. The other is the importance of time, or the sense of permanence that characterizes love.

To the proponents of marriage the love criterion is faulty because it thinks only of the couple. It exaggerates their independence of all else and creates what I will call a "we-selfishness." It is one thing to value the love between persons most highly and quite another to see them, as it were, isolated from their deeds, their family, and their society. The couple is very much what they actually do with one another and what they have become in relation to family and community. Those who believe love is enough to warrant intercourse are not merely denying the value of public, solemn ceremony; they are likewise denying that family and society have any substantial stake in the partners' serious love.

The more fundamental issue between the love and marriage criteria is that of life-commitment. Should sexual intercourse be restricted to a single person one loves enough to want to live a whole life with, and therefore marry, or should it be permitted to real but lesser loves? The argument of the love proponents against the consent criterion was that the ultimate act ought not to be commonly available but reserved for the ultimate relationship. To the marriage advocates this principle now substantiates their view. A love in which the lovers see their futures as inseparable is far more significant than one based mainly on the present. The latter love is precious and cherished, but it is surely not the deepest level of human relationship. This comes when each lover knows his own life can only reach fulfillment when lived out with his beloved. This represents as much value as human beings can attach to one another, and intercourse is obviously appropriate for them. Moreover, when reserved for this relationship, it continually signifies the unique worth the couple attaches to one another. It ennobles their love and strengthens their family ties. It enhances the sexual pleasures of their intercourse in terms of their exclusive personal intimacy.

From this more demanding perspective the love criterion seems more a concession to physical sexuality than a celebration of the highest love. Once one admits that love knows several levels—from friendship to love to "love for life"—to permit the most intimate of physical relations with people for whom one cares deeply, but not most deeply, seems a relaxation of personal concern. It is not so much the expression of love which has determined the standard as the desire to relax the standards for full sexual expression. The love criterion now appears less ethical than pragmatic, an effort at "a decent compromise" between consent, which makes intercourse too common, and marriage, which makes it so limited.

That somewhat hostile attitude to the love ethic is the indignant response of the marriage protagonists to the argument that marriage is less an ethical criterion for intercourse than love. From the marriage point of view that contention utilizes a double standard of judgment, comparing the best of one world with the worst of another. It contrasts sex in a deeply personal relationship, love, to that in an utterly impersonal, legal one, marriage. Since persons are of greater value than institutions, love is the more appropriate standard for intercourse. Yet why should marriage be seen only in its older, culturally rigidified form of a fixed pattern of role expectations? The proper comparison is not between those who care but have no license and those who don't care but are licensed. It is rather between intercourse in the context of "love for now" or "love for as long as we live." The advocates of marriage are not insisting on magic words to legitimate sex, but on a level of love so high that the partners will want to pledge the rest of their lives to one another.

Only after the intrinsic values have been clarified can the major prudential factor find a proper place. There is only one situation in which an unexpected pregnancy is not a moral trauma, and that is marriage. Even in marriage conception may come at an inconvenient time or be a grave, perhaps unwanted burden. Yet it does not fundamentally change that which bound the couple, one to the other. Their vow to the future most clearly included a willingness to have children. (So in Roman Catholicism the mental reservation of either party in a marriage not to have children is grounds for an annulment.) By any of the other standards conception upsets the primary assumption that the partners will enjoy sex together but not have children. Marriage may then occur to renew the relationship; childbirth or abortion may make it possible once again, if the girl is still willing to take the risks, but the special scars will remain. Marriage is the only situation which can humanly hope to cope with an accidental pregnancy. In that sense, despite our faith in technology and our proficiency, it is the only situation in which sexual relations can take place in full personal freedom. This may sound negative, but considering the number of abortions and forced weddings each year, it is not unrealistic.

There is a somewhat curious thought related to this. By the

love standard, it has been argued, intercourse might take place when love is sensed and present but not, as can happen, when it is momentarily gone. The marriage criterion is in this sense far freer. Since the married couple are bound to one another for life, they may in such moments of emptiness legitimately seek to find one another in the act of intercourse. Sometimes the deed is father to the feeling; making love restores the sense of love. What they were waiting for now reappears and justifies their reaching out to one another in such intimacy. Yet even if it does not, they have not violated what they know they mean to one another, for marriage is founded on the pledge to perse-vere together through the crises that may arise. The momentary absence of love is one of these. Trusting in love's return, pledged to see each other through such moments, they seek to restore the living sense of their relationship by making love. As long as their faith in what they will yet mean to one another gives substance to their marriage vows, their act must be adjudged ethical.

The advocates of the love criterion misunderstand this point. Intercourse without specific personal motivation seems by their standards always to be unethical. If they are thinking of that older sense of marital roles in which the wife existed to do her husband's sexual bidding whether she wished to or not, they are right. He has no right to exploit her. (Nor in these days of sexual equality does she have any right to make exorbitant sex-ual demands on him.) This point, however, deals more with cul-tural lag than increasing social reality. Few men try in an era of personalism to revive a legalistic, male-dominated sense of mar-riage so they can make their wives their sexual slaves. Few edu-cated women will tolerate it. This situation of married intercourse not preceded by high emotion is hardly coercion. Neither partner exploits; each seeks the other, hoping through the sexual act to bring to the surface the deep personal bond they know unites them. That sounds impersonal, hence, unethical. Yet it is a legitimate part of a relationship pledged to permanence, as long as their trust in each other mandates a commitment to continuity together. Thus, where the love criterion is liberating by allow-ing possibly for intercourse with several people in the course of a lifetime, the marriage ethic is far more flexible sexually in terms of the realities of an ongoing relationship.

If the discussion is extended in terms of society's and not just the individual's benefit, one may give both positive and negative reasons for the marriage standard. The monogamous marriage, for all its problems, is one of the great accomplishments of civilization. It has channeled to humanly valuable ends a sexual energy which when left free to indulge itself has been a major cause of social decay and degeneration. Confining sexual intercourse to marriage may cause some personal hardship under the present conditions of maturation, but they are modest compared to the difficulties society would inevitably face if sexual relations, even with proficient contraception, were the approved standard. If the love standard is the most ethical one, it should hold true after marriage. One, however, gets accustomed to one's spouse, and it becomes easier with time to fill in some of the emotional gaps left even in the best of marriages through a real but partial love of one another. When one adds to this the adventurous possibility of new sexual experiences, the chance of having several loves is not unreasonable. In any case, the love standard ultimately legitimates adultery. With it, the exclusiveness and trust that strengthened the marriage even in its difficult periods tend to dissolve. Doubt and uncertainty weaken it. A family that needs every support against a difficult civilization loses a major one. Not only the couple but society is the loser by a standard that makes such loosening of the marital vows possible.

The love advocates have suggested some practical and theoretical alternatives. The difficulty caused by two standards for intercourse might be overcome by employing them at different times. When a person is unmarried, he should live according to the love standard. Once he marries, that act should signify a shift to the sexual exclusiveness of the traditional marriage. A person should not consider himself ready for marriage until he feels confident he can adopt the new standard and live by it. Indeed, having been free to learn and experiment in his youth, he will find it easier to make a mature and responsible de-

cision for marriage and sexual exclusiveness. Surely such shifting of ethics in new contexts is what we expect of people in other
areas of their lives. We ask them not to fight as children, to kill
as soldiers and be nonviolent as adults. When we are young, we
play for fun and little is at stake; cheating is not so great a sin.
When we are older, the stakes are higher, and we play for
keeps; cheating is then criminal. Youth is almost expected to
squander money and energy, but not adulthood. Similarly, a
modern society should be more responsive to sex among young
adults, yet protect marriage by making it a time of exclusive
sexual relations. There are many signs that our society is in fact
moving in that direction.

One might further that view with another suggestion. Let it
be granted that intercourse is the ultimate act of personal relationship and is therefore appropriate only to persons who are
married. However, the new techniques of contraception make
possible a distinction between intercourse to express love and
intercourse for conception. Procreative intercourse is the more
ultimate act, and it alone, therefore, need be reserved for marriage. Intercourse with contraception is not as climactic. Hence,
while it is right with all those one loves, one should not have to
be married to participate in it.

There is a sense in which separating intercourse for love from
that for conception might help strengthen marriage. We take
it for granted that a couple contemplating marriage ought to
test their social compatibility. We encourage them to spend much
time together under varied circumstances to learn whether it is
likely they could live together in happiness. Despite such familiarity it is not uncommon for newlyweds working out their sexual
adjustment to discover that they are not well mated. This is
not simply a matter of physical or bodily adjustment but is,
rather, deeply personal. There is hardly an area of personality
as revealing as one's sexual behavior. But under the present
forms of permitted intimacy, that remains hidden from the person himself and from his beloved. Surely everything that can be
done in advance of marriage to limit the likelihood of divorce
should be done. Contraceptive (as against procreative) inter-

course should therefore be encouraged among couples who are seriously getting to know one another for it is an essential means of determining their compatibility.

A final rejoinder must also be considered. If love which is pledged for life validates intercourse, then it should be permitted to engaged couples. While they have not completed their vows or sworn to them in terms of their most cherished beliefs, they have nonetheless formally and publicly testified to their intention to undertake marriage together. Since their intercourse is permitted because of their commitment to marry, it could not later become a justification of adultery. On the other hand, in an age where marriage is long delayed and contraception is available, it would permit them to mitigate the sexual repressiveness of the present social arrangements.

The marriage protagonists are not persuaded by these arguments. They believe separate standards for procreative and contraceptive intercourse are an impractical and unrealistic idea. Obviously, begetting life is a far more ultimate act than making love, but it cannot be understood to exist in isolation. For most couples who practice any form of birth control, procreative intercourse is a rarity in terms of their total sex life together. When it does take place, therefore, it draws a good deal of its significance from the many acts of loving intercourse which have preceded it. There is an integrity to the sexual intercourse of a married couple which cannot be divided in so arbitrary a way between the procreative and the loving. To do so, if an exaggeration may be permitted, does not make the procreative act special, since nothing in it is changed. Rather it is the breaking of the rhythm or pill cycle or whatever, which becomes the ultimate act of love. If this division were taken seriously and adultery were limited to extramarital procreative intercourse, that would substantially change the meaning of the married couple's regular sexual relations because they would lose their exclusivity. That objection requires no further clarification.

The suggestion of using different criteria at different times of life is more practical, yet similarly unconvincing. It would inevitably put marriage in a dreadful light. The criterion for the youthful years, love, is by its openness and immediate concerns quite naturally, even physiologically, appealing. When marriage does come, it appears therefore precisely as a restrictive arrangement. After marriage let one begin an involvement with someone quite attractive and what stands in the way of a delightful culmination is, in contrast to the sex of youth, the marriage vows. Marriage becomes a hindrance to sexual self-expression. Legitimizing two kinds of experience, one less, one more restricting, is bound to make marriage seem less a continuing search for a relationship in ultimate depth than a species of repression imposed on people who want to have children together. This makes marriage a far more legalistic affair than does the present effort at a single, marital standard for sex. Thus, while adultery is barred in this two-step arrangement, even where it does not occur, the concept of marriage itself already creates a handicap for the couple.

One might see the present difficult social situation of marriage as deriving from something like the love standard. Marriage is called upon to justify itself in terms of the youthful rushes of feeling and excitement it produces. It is supposed to exist for passion and pay off in ecstasy. When in time its familiarity breeds frustration and irritation, it seems useless, almost a betrayal. Sometimes that does not mean love is dead but rather that the relation now operates in another, less sensational, though more continuous, way. Even a short separation from one another or a vacation together away from the usual burdens and routines will show that. Yet, despite such short-term therapies, the person who believes that love commends itself essentially by its youthful appearance will inevitably find marriage disappointing. He may then divorce or philander or do both continually in hope of regaining the old glandular arousal. He is pursuing the fantasy of youth eternal. His tragedy is not to have learned that mature love is fulfilled in sustaining a relationship over the years, rather than in the joys of only finding or beginning one. That is the difficulty society leads us to by suggesting that youthful visions of love and sexuality are more appropriate to personal fulfillment than lasting marriages grown rich in understanding and devotion.

The suggestion that experience of intercourse before marriage will forestall many divorces again seems to exaggerate the sexual act at the expense of the personal context in which it takes place. While there is obviously such a thing as simple sexual incompatibility, it would seem, particularly because of the change in general sexual attitudes, to be less and less the cause of post-marital difficulties in adjustment than it was in more repressive days. Sex is rather the arena in which more fundamental personal problems appear which are less likely to appear before marriage. There, as both partners are aware, less is at stake. One has not already committed one's entire existence to a relationship with only this person. It is in matters involving the greatest risk that tensions come to the surface. As long as one can always move on to another relationship, one can put up with a good deal in the present relationship and carry on quite a masquerade. When permanence is involved and one's whole life hangs on the outcome, the situation is quite different.

Couples moving toward marriage should get to know one another's sexual attitudes. Some physical intimacies seem appropriate to those on the brink of marriage. Such intimacies may not provide complete sexual knowledge of one another, but what they lose in foreknowledge will later be surpassed by awareness that the sexual relationship they have created between themselves is a most intimate sign of their exclusivity to one another. Not having overemphasized intercourse before marriage, they may be able to assign it its proper role afterward. It is not the mutual giving of orgasm which validates their marriage but the meaning they have for one another as persons, which includes, among many other things, their sexuality. This insistence on the preeminence of the personal should give them grounds for patience with one another as they learn to make love and a willingness to seek professional help should they encounter problems in this important aspect of their total love.

Furthermore, the engagement suggestion does not follow its argument through to a logical conclusion. If acts and pledges are taken seriously, why not wait until they are completed? Indeed, if this relationship is to be one for life, one should be all the more concerned to give it the highest regard and treat it with the utmost moral scrupulousness. For there remains a difference between engagement and marriage. The one may be broken with relative ease though not without pain. That is its purpose, to bring greater assurance to the vows undertaken in the marriage itself. Only then does the intention become deed and the lives become truly linked. This is why the full weight of the spiritual attestation is saved for the marriage ceremony itself. Validating intercourse by engagement is primarily, then, a concession to the sexual pressures and delays of our society. Rather than demean the significance of the marriage vows even in part, we should better put our energies into changing our society's sexual tone and making more youthful marriages emotionally and financially possible. Permitting intercourse during the period of engagement preceding marriage will mean little to those who are calling for a sexual revolution, but it is one more symptom indicating that we do not take the marriage vows with full seriousness.

The Jewish experience is of some interest here, since a major control of premarital sex during much of the postbiblical era was a betrothal, which came some time before what, by our standards, would be a youthful marriage. There is a continuous record of persons so pledged having intercourse before the wedding. In some few communities this or lesser intimacies seem almost to have been customary. Wherever such intercourse had taken place, no penalty was imposed upon the couple. One might even think to see here a survival of that older practice that the act of intercourse itself was a means of performing marriage.[83] However, these observations miss the point. While the premarital intercourse of the betrothed carried no legal penalties, the religious authorities considered the behavior immoral, decried it in exaggerated terms, demanded that the couples immediately marry, and did everything in their power to have communities put a stop to the practice. Though betrothal had substantial legal form, though it required a sort of divorce to break and put the woman under the laws concerning adultery, though its pledges were solemn in tone and socially attested, the rabbis considered not waiting until the marriage itself had taken place a highly indecent act. This was in part because even in the earlier centuries of this era one might no longer marry a woman merely by the act of intercourse but had to do so in a special context of rite and vow. Without the full pledging, the rabbis insisted, intercourse of the betrothed was unethical, though they would not impose a legally enforceable penalty for it.

It should not be necessary, after all that has been said, to elucidate the special responsibilities which this marriage ethic imposes. Yet this section of the discussion cannot end without indicating that this vigorous statement of the marital view has been strongly attacked and bitterly rejected. The advocates of the other positions have a major retort that is blunt but effective: The marriage standard is exactly what has been tried for years and has not worked. It did not keep people from premarital intercourse or adultery in former times. It will do so less and less today. A standard that will not be observed is senseless. To tell young people to wait until they are married to have intercourse seems increasingly ridiculous. Marriage is important, and intercourse for the sake of having children should be confined to a marriage so there can be stable families. The real questions are, How can one dare to suggest further repression of man's sexual nature for the most vital years of his life? or, Why must the love which justifies sexual intercourse be a love of such intensity it calls forth the lifelong commitment of the lovers? The former position says sex is too important to people, particularly the young, to restrict it to marriage. The latter says love is precious enough to live one's present by, including sexual relations, and it should not have to extend into the far future to justify its activities.

Each position has its strengths. None is without serious weaknesses. At least now the values involved should be clearer. Except that knowing what each criterion emphasizes is not the same as deciding which one you want to accept and live by. That you must decide for yourself—by trying to make up your mind what you think about egoism, about sex, about being a person, about love, and about marriage. I have given you the alternatives as best I understand them and tried to put each of them in the best possible light. Now that I have helped you face the various options quite directly, I have an obligation to carry the discussion into an area that I have tried to keep out of the material discussed thus far—what I myself have decided after reflection and self-examination.

Conclusion

10

SPEAKING PERSONALLY

By this time, I assume you have gained sufficient distance from me not to take what I say for granted, nor to disagree with me solely because I am a rabbi and older. If your needs for dependency or rebellion are reasonably well in hand, my views should help you summarize your own, whether in the direction of agreement or dissent.

I begin with a sense of outrage at the sexual tone of our civilization. For all the positive activities today between the sexes, there is all about us an unnatural, sick concentration on sex that is surely contagious. I suppose no age has ever been without serious sexual temptations. The rabbis speak of the prevalence of prostitutes, and Jewish medieval literature regularly ponders the difficulties occasioned by adultery and incest. Still it is difficult to find a comparable age when sex was prompted not just by physiology and neighborhood but by the continual pressure of the combined forces of the civilization. Today almost everything is suffused with sex, and the mass media, serving an exploitative economic apparatus, keep sex continually before us. Then, in a pious mood, society says, "Wait until marriage." The titillation is constant, but the ideals remain supposedly quite pure; this is the real obscenity of our time.

Moreover, we are continually being told that the modern, the advanced people of our time are already utilizing a newer, a freer sexual ethic. They are rebelling against the old repressiveness and are expressing themselves more fully, because more naturally. At its extreme, a whole way of life is involved. To live means to have fun. To be youthful means to gather new and exotic experiences. Everything should be tried, and sex is no different from travel or restaurants. And this is no esoteric theory, but the mood that prevails on many a campus, as in many a bar or resort. This is the sophisticated attitude of our time. To ask serious questions about it, much less to want to think these values through is to mark oneself as odd or square or both. Even if someone asks you what you seriously believe about sex, the chances are that is a come-on for analysis and refutation to show how advanced he is and how old-fashioned you are. The name of the game is freer-than-thou. In such a milieu, who can talk about ethics, much less about God? If you believe anything, you learn to keep it well hidden. Most of us are really Marranos.

In such a social context I feel a great sense of compassion and admiration for anyone who, despite the prodding, the hypocrisy, the lechery, the confusion about him, is determined to be as thoughtful about his sex life as he can be. No matter which of the standards he accepts for himself, I honor him for refusing to surrender as a self-determining person to our vulgarizing society. I hope this book has strengthened him in that resolve. This, more than any rule I could suggest about sexual behavior, is what will count in the long run.

I wish it were possible for me to ease his burdens by pointing out to him the single, unambiguous ethical truth. However, and this must be added to all the other difficulties of being a man of integrity today, our ethical situation itself is confused and complicated. Men of another age faced their temptations with greater certainty than we can. When conscience appeared among men and the Bible was widely considered sacred, adultery, prostitution, and nonmarital relationships were forbidden. People knew this was right, and they were not troubled in that faith. They occasionally transgressed and felt guilty, but the standards, at least, were clear. No Job ever arose to argue the standards of sexual morality or any other ethical command with God.

We have a more disturbing form of guilt today: we feel we ought to know what is right, but we cannot be sure we do. No single standard regulating sex or most other serious human problems is without question. Inevitably several views com-

pete for our assent, each backed by strong arguments, with even
the most appealing not free from serious criticism. And since
they are always partially contradictory, there is no way of accepting them all or combining the best of this with the best of
that to avoid the problems of both. So we modern men, even
when we feel as certain as we can, always leave a little room for
doubt, for questions, for new knowledge, for a new approach.
We can only make a choice for the time being, or insofar as we
know. We may have to stake our lives on these commitments—
in many issues, like marriage, not to take the whole risk is to
give an answer worth nothing—but we abhor fanaticism and are
leery of martyrdom. Basically we cannot be that certain. So
our decisions are not absolute but the best we have been able to
come up with. Our convictions are not without question, but
this, as far as we can tell, is where we stand and who we are.

Such open certainty is not limited to modern secularists or
liberal religionists. Being fundamental to the modern temper it
affects religious orthodoxies as well. The Roman Catholic church
may still claim to give infallible dogmatic guidance and have a
God-given power to instruct the faithful in matters of faith and
morality. Yet today it is greatly agitated over priestly celibacy,
which is only a human, if ecclesiastic, rule, and birth control, in
which conscience directs many against the official teaching. An
Orthodox Jew will accept the rulings of the great legal masters
of our day as the contemporary equivalent of the Torah God gave
Moses on Sinai. Yet he can ask why in the face of radically
changed conditions the contemporary practice should not follow
the suggestions of Jacob Emden, Jacob Toledano, and Zeev Falk
and permit the *pilegesh* relationship. When orthodoxies include a doctrine of inner development, they are far more open,
despite their certainty, than were their predecessors a century
ago. At present this is, of course, the chief charateristic of
religious liberals who believe God's will is always understood
through the fallible and finite perceptions of man.

Thus, even one who does decide to approach sexual matters
ethically can only hope to reach a limited certainty. This is not
much—yet the concern for even this sort of standard is enough

to cut us off from the lazy and indulgent and make us
stand against our society's sick sexuality. This is not an easy time
in which to try to be truly human.

From that and much else that I have said it should be apparent that I do not see how I can declare that only one of the three
criteria remaining before us is ethical. Depending on what you
believe about man's sexuality, about being a person, about marriage, each is somewhat convincing and ought to be accepted.
Yet that is logically impossible. We cannot at the same time have
the freedom of the mutual-consent ethics with the restrictions
of the love standard or the greater restriction demanded by the
marriage standard. What we require, therefore, is something
far more pluralistic, a ranking rather than a comprehensive
rule, a hierarchy rather than a single, synthesizing principle. I
am thinking of something like the rabbis' multileveled judgment of what constituted sexual misbehavior. Some acts, like
intercourse with one's betrothed, are forbidden, but once committed, the couple marries without penalty or official stigma.
Some acts, like adultery, are within human jurisdiction to
punish, but others, like incest, are left to God himself. Other
acts, like rape or seduction, are matters of community concern, while still others, such as intercourse between consenting
unmarried adults, are left to the domain of conscience. The rabbis, though they sought to serve God in their legal and moral
teaching, accepted a multiplicity of values in the variety of human behavior they knew men faced. This commends itself to
me as a model for working out an approach to premarital intercourse that is not overly simplistic.

You will recall that I found the healthy-orgasm criterion to
be ethically defective because it made possible the subordination
of one person's rights to that of the other. I believe—and
it is no less important to me because I know that it is a matter
of faith and not rationally demonstrable—that all persons
are of equal moral worth and must be treated as such. That tenet
of Judaism, which I affirm, makes it impossible for me to accept
the egoistic, healthy-orgasm ethic. Any standard that might be

used to invalidate the moral dignity of another person, I cannot consider ethical.

This rejection indicates why I must give some ethical status to the mutual-consent criterion. Here there is concern for both partners, as each is required to bring his free, responsible assent to the act. This is an obvious ethical advance over permitting any form of coercion or exploitation in the name of self.

Yet more must be said. The very commitment to persons which made this position more ethical than that of healthy orgasm now makes it unsatisfactory as well. This standard is interested in only two aspects of the person, his will and his sexuality. Sex being good, a person is asked only to be a proper moral agent in undertaking it. In an almost Kantian sense, if his intention is right, if the act would be right for others in a similar situation and he treats his partner with dignity, the deed is validated. But this means man's moral function has somehow been isolated from all the rest of him. Who he is in his fullness, what the other means to him as a person and not just as free decision-maker, is not central to the judgment. Surely in sexual matters, where feelings and emotions are most intimately part of the central act—generally the immediate reasons for it—to limit the judgment only to the moral decision of parties is not to ask enough of them. Here emphatically a person is more than glands and will. A good deal of what we are as men is how we relate in fullness to other people.

In this insistence on fullness my Jewish concern for the moral dignity of persons has been extended by Martin Buber's teaching on what it means to be a whole person. Buber made a by now famous distinction between I–it and I–thou situations. An "it" is not truly a person; a "thou," someone addressed in the singular, as an individual, in terms of who he himself fully is, is a real person. For the most part, we are treated by others as "its." They are interested only in part of us—our clothes, our personality, our money, our status. They care for us largely in terms of what we can do for them or how they can use us. They do not relate to us as a whole person, as what we come to know we can be when someone does reach out to us from his depths and meets us in our own depths, as in friendship or love. That is how we know what it means to be a real person and why it is wrong to settle for anything less. The old Kantian concerns for the moral will may be a start toward full personal relationship, but in the I–thou alone can we see it consummated. To put it somewhat crudely, the only human contact demanded under the consent criterion is first of wills and then of genitals. This makes too little of man and allows sexual relations to be another activity where he is seen in terms of his parts rather than summoned to full human interrelationship. Here, of all acts, where man and woman are to be physically and emotionally in the closest unity, it would seem reasonable that they should be expected to be in the most genuine personal contact as well. If they are not concerned with each other as persons but only as sex partners, they are treating each other as "its" and thus, despite their free consent to the intercourse, are being unethical to each other as full human beings. How much truer the act would be if their sexual activity arose from what they meant to one another, if sex were not the reason for their intercourse but rather the natural outgrowth of all that they shared with one another. There is a radical difference between loving someone because he is sexy and having sex with someone because of your love.

I am far more concerned with the personal meaning of intercourse than with its physiological or psychological virtues because I believe one's body should, wherever it is reasonable, serve the whole self rather than the self be a servant to the body, though the two are obviously indivisible. Thus Jewish tradition made it a duty for a person to be concerned for his health. He must eat regularly, fast only in moderation, see a doctor when sick, and bathe to keep clean. Yet narcissism or devotion to the physical for its own sake is not strong in the Jewish ethos. The same is true with sex. Judaism made marriage, regular intercourse, and having children primary religious commandments reinforced by intense community concern. But, it would have made no sense to believing Jews to suggest that accumulating orgasms was admirable, or that mastering every position for intercourse was a virtuosity worth pursuing. The closest one comes to such attitudes in Judaism is the man blessed in the number of his sons or the woman admired for her many children.[84] A direct concern with sexual fulfillment is fundamentally physiological and egoistic, and probably quite impersonal, even though it may care about giving as well as getting sensation. The linkage of intercourse with marriage, however, concentrates on the human value of the sex, its significance for the family, the Jewish people, and therefore, human history.

Man is much more than his sexuality. That is what Judaism knew and Martin Buber helps us understand more deeply. Anyone who shares this high estimate of what it means to be a full person can hardly be satisfied with sexual relations based merely on consent.

Two standards which speak of the partners acting as whole persons have previously come before us. The one made friendship, the other, love, the necessary condition for the consent. The friendship criterion calls for what may be termed the "minimum personal relationship," because it wants to maximize the possibilities of ethical intercourse. The love criterion puts the emphasis on the personal relationship, and by demanding that much of the partners, limits substantially the possibility of ethical intercourse. The choice between them seems almost entirely to depend on how one balances one's need for intercourse against the need to be a full person.

I think highly of friendship, but sexual intercourse seems to me a rather extravagant way in which to express it. One should think so much of self and what his most intimate physical giving of self means, that he should not do so without the most worthwhile reason. Or, to put it more positively, I value intercourse too highly as an interhuman experience for me to find it an appropriate act with a person who is only a friend.

Socially, the problem in being fully human today is less a lack of sexual outlets than the insistence that we price ourselves cheaply as persons. To invest friendship with all the physical intimacies of love is to give fully in an essentially limited situation.

Society continually asks us to make that bargain, to spend ourselves extravagantly but not make too many personal demands
in return. We are early taught that love and compassion, individual attention and personal concern are too much to expect in
our busy society, so acceptingly we learn to live without them.
This is where the social revolution must begin. If we are persons,
we must fight to be persons—and not just for ourselves alone
but to make our entire society more humane. In sex I believe this
means that intercourse should at least be reserved for those whom
we love and not extended to one with whom we simply share
friendship.

I think this high sense of the meaning persons ought to have
for one another was implicit in the one nonmarital sexual relationship Judaism tolerated, the *pilegesh*. This was no temporary affair of two friends spending occasional nights or week-
ends together. In the small, medieval world they lived together
in the man's home, in a community where everyone might be
expected to know what was going on. They were legally man
and "demi-wife." Our sources do not speak of their love, yet when
we remember that in those prepill days children would most
likely result from this arrangement, it is difficult to see so much
structure and stability as a kind of friendship rather than of
love. While the legal authorities ultimately did away with the
pilegesh, apparently for ethical reasons, it did not so outrage
their moral sensibilities that it was immediately intolerable.
Some of the rabbis accepted it, and not merely, I feel, because
the biblical precedents were so strong. Matters more fundamental
to Jewish law have been reversed by rabbinic edict when the authorities felt it essential to do so. It seems more reasonable to
assume that the lenient thinkers sensed some element of human
decency in it, perhaps as against other possible nonmarital
sexual activities, and this allowed them to tolerate it. This experience says something to me about the love as against the
friendship criterion. If you will recall, I argued that the
friendship standard is more ethical than the mere consent criterion because it is truer to what it means to be a person. Now
I must take that a step further. The love criterion is more fully

ethical still because it is more fully personal. That is its great appeal.

Need much be said about the value of love in a day when it has become practically the only unquestioned virtue, for many the only real faith? Love opens us to a sense of personal depth and quality we rarely find elsewhere in our civilization. It calls us to a life of richer meaning and value than anything our culture regularly sets before us. To share true love is to make life worthwhile, to make existence a privilege. In a society which specializes in exploitation and manipulation, in an era where despair and anxiety are characteristic, love is the most precious of accomplishments.

I do not see how I can deny the ethical quality of sexual acts that arise from and bespeak a genuine love—and it is much too late in the discussion to raise tedious cavils about self-deception and the need to make certain. Love more than any other experience commonly known to men exalts us from bestiality to humanity, from being used, to being ourselves. For people who truly love, to express that love in sexual relations cannot be called unethical. Particularly when contrasted to the human reality of most of what we do with other people whom we say we love, any love-making which is true to the love between us, even if we are unmarried, is right.

Yet I want to carry my pluralism a step further. Though I esteem love greatly, I believe men can reach an even more significant level of personal existence. Ordinary love is wonderful for the present, perhaps for the past as well. It does not work too well for the future, for it tends to go as it came. That is what, for all its preciousness, makes it ordinary love. But a person must live his life not only in the present, if he would be a self, but into and through the future as well. Man is more than moments of meaning. He is that integrity of self which carries on from birth to death. Because we know or fear time will make love end, we want to extract ourselves from the continuing flow of time, and withdraw from life as continuity. To do that is to lose true identity. If men only knew love-for-now, then they might have to deny time and content themselves with such oasis moments in the wilderness of existence. They know better, because they have more enduring loves. Indeed, every ordinary love takes on great joy at its inception because of the hope that it will be what we have always known we wanted, a lifelong love, one that will fill our lives not merely in the present but in all the future. Consequently, when such loves occur, they seem bigger than life, or as the Song of Songs puts it, "Love is stronger than death." [85] This is less a romantic exaggeration than the acknowledgment of the most meaningful possible human situation.

To affirm and uplift a person for a time is no small thing in our world, but to love him for life and be loved in return is to make both persons, finally, fully what they might be. Great daring is required to bind one's future to another's.

I hasten to add that it makes no difference if this love later does not turn out to be rich enough to endure. Without taking risks there can be no authentic existence. In taking them we sometimes fail. The most important measure of success is responding honestly to the situation confronting us, not in always being right. Jewish experience shows that cherishing marriage and accepting the occasional necessity for divorce are not incompatible, at least in the sort of community the Jews created.

I find this sense of the distinction between love and love for all one's life missing from most of the contemporary discussions of love, sex, and marriage. This absence is particularly notable among the advocates of the new morality who talk so much about the personal.[86] I think the uniform value attached to every variety of love derives from the feeling that our times are poor in love, even in its more modest manifestation, friendship. In such an underprivileged culture ordinary love is as much a source of value as most people can aspire to. Yet I see this failure to make distinctions reflecting something else, and I know that this particular insight of mine comes from my sharing Judaism's intense concern with history. Being satisfied with love-for-now rather than reaching for lifelong love seems a highly significant example of one of the great moral tragedies of our time: the devaluation of the future in the name of the present. We focus so sharply on ourselves in the here and now, that we have less and less concern for our continuity into what will yet be. We withdraw from the forward flow of historic time to try to pack the present as full of experience as we can. To be alive has come to mean the intensification of now. The moment that passes without high sensation or immediate self-validation is the equivalent of death. This style seems appropriate to our paradoxical historical situation. Life seems our chief good, and we have made great progress in extending and enriching it. Yet we all know that the military means exist, now, and by human will, to destroy us all. In a world where the plague is conquered and the West knows no famine, the bomb remains agonizingly real. Though we bury it deep lest we think of it, the concept of annihilation pervades the unconscious of modern civilization. Since we cannot be certain of a future, we want to live in the present. I think that explains much of the live-for-now mood of our time, in sex as in other things.

Affluence is another factor. Most of us are not yet so financially secure that we can abandon the future and spend now. Still, jobs and money will probably be available in the future, so to borrow from it to live in the present is a logical idea. And that is what we do when we move the criterion for intercourse forward from love-for-life to love-for-now, much less to momentary sensation.

If our culture has particular reasons for thinking of sexual relations in terms of the present, the single most conducive social context for adopting that point of view is to be found at the university. The student is old enough to act as an adult, but we do not yet expect him to undertake full adult obligations, though many students do make a serious effort to expand their responsibilities. The normal individual knows his future is mortgaged to this institution for four years at least, hence, he will not worry very much about the life to come until he is about to graduate. In the interim he has the heavy responsibility of staying in school and doing well there. What time he has for himself is understandably devoted to enjoying the present. Besides, everyone else in this campus world is his peer, and they too are trying to take advantage of this breathing space. The older students become missionaries of the joys of immediacy, urging the neophytes to use the quickly passing pre-squaredom years to explore and experiment. The faculty, too, almost always focuses more sharply on what is wrong with accepted values than on what is reasonably certain to remain true for the rest of one's life. So one is almost irresistibly taken with the belief that youth is the best time of life, the model for what adulthood ought to be. There is a powerful temptation to believe that only what gives satisfaction in the here and now is worthy of pursuit. Thus love may authorize, but it should not bind or project the lovers' responsibilities into the future. Since most people rarely choose a sex ethic but adopt one from the group they want to be associated with, the move from home to school often involves a sexual crisis, though every campus has more conscientious objectors than libertines.

The university, because it provides a sheltered environment to a select community in the in-between years from adolescence to adult responsibility, is the social center of the love ethic for sexual intercourse.

This analysis has been deliberately overstated in the hope of making a point that is often strongly resisted. I believe—again my Jewish faith asserts itself—that man can only be man through time and in responsibility. Becoming a whole person must include not just what one is and can enjoy but equally the enduring relationships and continuing commitments through which alone one can mature. The friendships which increase in understanding as in demand, the love that deepens to obligate as to quicken us over the years, these are what make men fully human. Integrity of self is not merely the work of moments or periods but the hard-won result of pursuing a continuity in our lives. Momentary genuineness is splendid, but we have not become true persons unless we can extend occasional authenticity to a lifetime of trying to be true. Experiment has its place, and joy must not be underrated. Still it is in what we do with our lives in the long run that we show how human we are. Marriage and a family are not an eventual necessity—an attitude that invites disaster before the vows are spoken!—but the preferred path of personal fulfillment. Without their intense commitment, demanding trust, unrelenting involvement, it is difficult to become fully human. They are worth working and waiting for, and this includes cultivating the values and attitudes that can make it possible for them to succeed.

Let me illustrate the difference between these two attitudes toward life by proposing a choice between two possible situations. Neither is really satisfactory, yet they represent what life offers to many people. In one case we will find love, rich and moving, but never great enough to result in marriage. Thus, while such affairs last months or even years, each inevitably ends, and the lovers go their separate ways. The other possibility is of a life spent in a marriage but one not initiated because of love. The couple has very genuine regard for one another, but it cannot be said to rise to that level of empathy and passion we call love. Yet knowing themselves to be unlikely to have a much richer emotional experience or to have a better partner with whom to spend their lives, they marry. Would you prefer a life of love that never comes to marriage over a life of marriage that knows regard but not love? The choice is, of course, odious, and one should not be forced into such an undesirable situation. Yet many people are. I like that choice no better than anyone else because I feel that life is best fulfilled in love-for-life and, therefore, marriage. Yet, seen from the perspective of time and of a whole life, if there must be a choice, then being married, even only in deep friendship, seems to me far more personally significant than being in love from time to time. If forced to choose, I confess I am not ultimately a romantic who thinks high moments are more important than continual personal growth. I value ecstasy, but I believe in almost every case becoming a person is more truly bound up with perseverance.

Thus, the most ethical form of human relationship I know is love-for-life. Its appropriate social and religious structure is the monogamous marriage. This being so, marriage is, if I may use the strange formulation of ethical pluralism, the most right context, that is, the best criterion for the validity of sexual intercourse. And I think every human being should try to reach the highest possible level of ethical behavior.

It is one of the besetting evils of our time that many people are satisfied to be "somewhat" ethical. "Doing the best I can" becomes an excuse for retaining self-indulgent bad habits. "I have to give in to myself every once in a while" or "I'm only human" is generally a rationalization for moral sloth or ethical unconcern. How easily the phrases become a philosophy, and what was an excuse becomes a way of life. I believe, as Judaism has taught, that to be a full human being means to strive continually for moral excellence and to make moral excellence not only the ideal framework but the increasing reality of one's existence. I am not saying that if you are not a saint you are not human—though I do not understand why people should consider it somehow more human not to be a saint (in Judaism, a righteous man). I am not saying everyone ought to spend his time morbidly worrying about whether he has been excellent in his behavior toward others—though I think the central importance of moral concern is often overlooked. I am saying that to settle for anything less than the highest possible ethical standards for our lives is already to compromise our humanity. There is plenty of time, after the act, to speak of our humanity and acknowledge our limitations. If we mean it sincerely, if that confession gives us the courage to resume our high standards as we face the next decision, Judaism then insists God himself will forgive and encourage us.

Every human being who knows his life is tied to those of all other men should want to live by the highest ethical standards. Most men, I am afraid, will be quite content to live by a modest morality or by none at all. Idealists must never forget how resistive to righteousness human nature is under all the fancy clothes and friendly etiquette. If the masses of men are not apt to act very ethically, then it is all the more important for the sensitive few to do as much as they can, to do the best deed for its own sake as well as for its example and benefit for all men.

I know what I am suggesting is not easy in our society, and I am pained with that thought. In any case, those who think as I do have an obligation to encourage people to marry young and to help them financially and emotionally to do so. One of our deepest sins is that we keep our youth so immature that, when they are biologically ripe for sex, they are hardly ready as persons for marriage. (Are they much readier for personalized intercourse without marriage?) Our new morality ought to begin by teaching us to see marriage, not love, as the place of human fulfillment. Then it ought to move on to demand that parents and, if necessary, the state, create the conditions—emotional and financial—which would make it practical. This would take a good deal of change in attitudes. I know no new morality which would not. It would not cure everything. But I know nothing that would, except, if I may say so, the coming of the Messiah. The best way of making that possible is for men who care about themselves and about mankind to do all they can to live by the highest ethical standards.

That surely has been the millennial concern of the Jewish people. It has stood for moral excellence not only on a personal level but in its community social style as well. Not every Jew has lived up to that high ideal, and many a Jewish community has been full of arrogance and contention. Yet over the centuries this people has remained surprisingly true to that ancient biblical vision of man and mankind ennobled. It has managed in the most diverse cultures, climates, economies, and social structures to convert its ancient dedication to moral excellence, to the more than moral excellence called holiness, into ways, habits, and disciplines that made prophetic values every man's way of life. Through this structuring of individual existence it helped each man fulfill himself and his people's destiny. As part of the Jew's stubborn continuity, he kept high standards of intellectuality, personal fidelity, and social concern before the world. And throughout the duration of the Jewish people he knew that his personal participation in the task of bringing mankind to its full human destiny would in the end of days be achieved.

I am saying that while every man should take the standards of moral excellence upon himself, the believing Jew has special reason to do so. That is the tradition of his people. Moreover, if he practices his Judaism as a member of its caring community, he will find in them as in it, continuing support and stimulus for his effort to settle for nothing less than the accomplishment of the highest moral good.

This statement will indicate to some that I have ended precisely where I began, affirming the Jewish tradition. I do not think that is what has happened. I have, for the most part, not spoken in terms of Judaism, so to others it will seem a matter for criticism that a student of Judaism neglected it in order to talk instead about being or becoming a whole person.

What I have tried to do in this analysis is to comprehend the problem in its contemporary setting and speak to those it concerns in their own language. Many of the most thoughtful things college students themselves say about sex ethics are put in terms of what it means to be a person. I imagine they think of that as a purely secular value. For me it is a matter of religious belief. I see it as a part of American secularism only because Christianity once dominated western culture and infused it with a concern for persons, though that idea was radically extended in the spread of Enlightenment rationalism and now in existentialist concerns. I do not see how secularism alone might validate such a fundamental faith in persons—all persons—today. What shows us that persons are so important that they should be the criterion of all ethical behavior? Science cannot prove "persons" exist distinct from bodies, much less that they have an intrinsic worth. Philosophy is badly split over whether persons are undemonstrable, and therefore an illogical assertion, or are a self-evident fact, which is therefore more a creed or dogma than an idea. Modern politics is interested in power; business, in profits; the social order, in privilege; most people, in personal benefit. Where will a faith in persons strong enough to power lives and transform society come from and how will it be sustained? Had I not believed in what Judaism has taught me about what it means to be a person, I could not have written as I have. I spoke to a universal problem in universal terms in order to be understood. But all that universalism is based on a quite particularly Jewish faith. One might perhaps have such a faith if one were not a Jew. But if one were not somehow in the Jewish family of religions or under their influence, I am no longer sure, in this radically skeptical world, how one would come by it. Thus, knowing how my particular Jewish faith authorizes every universal affirmation made about persons here, I would see this discussion as deeply Jewish and deeply human at the same time, precisely the mixture I think the faith of Judaism requires.

Yet, as this personalist-Jewish analysis proceeded, a double transformation took place. The old Jewish attitudes toward sexual relations could not be validated in as rigid and single-leveled a form as they had become in recent centuries. The pluralistic stance I have taken is more liberal because more personalistic than that known by traditional Judaism. At the same time, the personalist emphasis on the individual and the present seems intolerably narrow when seen from the Jewish concern with time and structure. In turn, this makes me far more restrictive than existentialists or new-morality protagonists would be.

Perhaps it will help—certainly it will help me—if now, even briefly, I use something more like my natural language, that of internal Jewish religious discourse, to say what I believe and what it implies for sexual conduct.

God, as best we understand Him, is not neutral but holy. We men, knowing Him, should try to bring that character of holiness into our lives. We are, when we are mature, free to do so, but we do not. This is the central problem of human history. By God's grace the Jews came as a people to know Him and understand itself as bound to Him and His service in history. This extraordinary but continual community experience of relationship, now dramatic, as at the mountains—Sinai, Carmel, and Zion—now everyday, as in the long centuries of biblical struggle to integrate this consciousness, changed this people's character. The Jews pledged themselves as a people, its individuals and its community alike, to live by God's demands on men. Further, it took upon itself obligations that went beyond what all men are required to do so that it would reflect the highest standards of human behavior and endure as a particular people dedicated to God's service in history. It vowed to live that way until all men should come to know that God so well that they too would transform their lives in terms of His reality. Generation after generation, the Jews renewed that promise, and now they and that service are inseparably intertwined. Though often, individually and as a community, they have failed to live up to that pact, God, they knew, never rejected them and their activity on His behalf. Rather, in the mysterious way in which He managed to give continuing order to the universe, He sustained the people of Israel and would not let it, as a whole, disappear from history until its task had been completed. This relationship of mutual love and obligation between God and the people of Israel, Jews call the Covenant.

The Covenant is carried out by the Jews when it is made the basis of their existence and thus applied to every aspect of life. (Any religious-secular dichotomy has, therefore, little meaning in Judaism.) Yet the Jewish community has found no more central and significant form for the individual Jew to live in that Covenant than his own personal covenant, marriage.[87] In its exclusiveness and fidelity it has been the chief analogy to the oneness of the relationship with God as the source of personal worth and development. In marriage's intermixture of love and obligation the Jew has seen the model of faith in God permeating the heart and thence all one's actions. Through his children he has found the greatest personal joy while carrying out the ancient Jewish pledge to endure through history for God's sake. Though he knows sex can be one of man's easiest ways to degradation, through the marriage covenant he has made it a chief means of serving God and becoming righteous. So he has always deplored sexual immorality as a sin against God and human dignity alike.

Today the Jew finds himself in a new social situation that presents him with a strange mixture of freedom and danger. He is marvelously at home in the non-Jewish world in a way he has never known. In his eagerness to become a part of it, motivated by his appreciation of its many virtues and eager to put far behind him any unnecessary and restrictive differences, many Jews have gone so far as to give up much of their old Jewish faith. At home now in a secular world such a Jew is not sure how much he believes in God and is therefore less certain of His Covenant with the Household of Israel. The average Jew's interest in Jewish religious practice is small, and his substitute for it is to be, simply, a decent person. He thinks society should be made much better and his surrogate for corporate Jewish religiosity is to support, in high statistical disproportion, almost every activity which seeks to do that.

In recent years the Jew has been quite concerned about the change in sexual attitudes. He still abhors adultery, for he knows it destroys the possibility of marriage as it ought to be, and he wants that and a loving family for himself and his children. The latter he knows will go on to a higher education and thus marry late. He is proud of the old Jewish sexual morality, but he sometimes wonders whether there is not something ethical about a young couple, really in love, having intercourse with one another, provided that they use contraceptives.

I think in this question as in many others he will have to consider whether the Jewish people, from whom he has gained and continues to gain so much, can long continue if it is satisfied only to try to be decent rather than struggle for moral excellence as a regular way of life. Jews who secularize the traditional terms of Jewish existence are ending its capacity to produce large numbers of men of value and are terminating its contribution to society. Those are secular goals. From the Jewish view they are breaking down Israel's Covenant with God. Ethical persons, in sexual as in other matters, are to be praised highly. But that is simply not good enough if human history as a whole is to be transformed and fulfilled. What we need today, as Judaism has always insisted in the past, is devotees of excellence in righteousness, that is, Jews, real Jews, devoted Jews, who will live the Covenant by sanctifying every aspect of their existence and most certainly their sexual behavior. Perhaps they will be a minority in the Jewish community today, as they occasionally were in the past. Yet I believe that there are such people in the American Jewish community today and that this faithful minority may once again be the most important part of this unusual people as it stubbornly continues on its messianic way. I do not know precisely what the details of such a sanctifying Covenant existence for every area of life would be like in this shifting modern world, nor do I think it easy in this civilization to stay for long on that level. Nonetheless, I believe much of the old Jewish life style is transferrable or adaptable to our situation, as I hope this discussion of sexual relations has manifested. I believe Jews who share this faith ought to have the courage to trust that, as we go forward in loyalty to that ancient Covenant, we shall, haltingly, find an authentic way to fulfill God's purposes in history with His help.

NOTES

1. Thoughtful researchers in this field are careful to make this distinction. See, for example, Robert R. Bell, *Premarital Sex in a Changing Society,* Prentice-Hall, Inc., Englewood Cliffs, N.J., 1966 (henceforth: *Premarital*), pp. 6-8, and Ira L. Reiss in "The Sexual Renaissance in America," ed. Reiss, *The Journal of Social Issues,* April 1966, Vol. XXII, No. 2 (henceforth: *Journal*), p. 136 f. Yet see below, note 6, for a discussion on the confusion between the two both in practice and in general effect.

2. Research in this area is still in its infancy, and both findings and methodology are in dispute. I have followed the data given in clear fashion by Bell, *Premarital,* pp. 56-58. At least two researchers have found the percentage of females having premarital relations to be far less than this, and one of them has not hesitated to see his study corroborating a general trend. Mervin B. Freedman studied a small group of girls during their four years in an Eastern college. Of these, 22 percent had engaged in intercourse during that period, almost always with men with whom they were emotionally deeply involved (see *The New York Times,* July 11, 1966, pp. 58-59). Nevitt Sanford did a similar study with girls at three widely separated schools. He felt it safe to generalize that about 20-30 percent of college women are not virgins by the time they graduate (see *Time,* April 9, 1965). A study by Seymour Halleck showed that 22 percent of all females questioned at the University of Wisconsin had had sexual relations, although 30 percent of all females questioned thought it was wrong (cited in *America,* June 10, 1967). By contrast, Gordon Blaine cited studies showing that by 1953 the proportion of women involved was 50 percent (approximately the general national average, according to Kinsey's middle-class, well-educated sample) and for men, 67 percent (well below Kinsey's national figure for males; see Bell, *Premarital,* p. 57, who puts the figures in context; for Blaine, see *Sex in America,* ed. Grunwald, Bantam Books, New York, 1964, p. 18).

3. That is one of the major theses of Bell's book. See *Premarital,*

p. 12, and the study and interpretation of the data, pp. 54-59. Similarly, Reiss, who is one of the enthusiastic advocates of a sexual morality that would be more permissive than society has heretofore held, admits that, while people believe there has been a big change in the practice of premarital intercourse, "the evidence from all the available major studies is in strong agreement that although *attitudes* have changed considerably during this period (last 20-25 years), many areas of sexual *behavior,* such as premarital coital rates, have not . . ." (Reiss, *Journal,* p. 126).

4. See Blaine, in *Sex in America,* ed. Grunwald, p. 19.

5. The data here are difficult to come by and interpret, since the marriage standards are undefined. The relevant Kinsey data and some of their interpretations are presented, somewhat tendentiously, by Richard Hettlinger in *Living with Sex: The Student's Dilemma,* The Seabury Press, New York, 1966, pp. 131-34. A discussion of the same material is given by Bell, *Premarital,* pp. 143-45, and for some cross-cultural data see Harold T. Christensen, "Scandinavian and American Sex Norms," in Reiss, *Journal,* p. 68, No. 8, and pp. 71 and 72.

6. To achieve a reasonably dispassionate climate in which to discuss sexual ethics is not easy. Researchers have often been subjected to pressures to prevent them from doing their work or making it known (see Bell, *Premarital,* p. 6, and Reiss, *Journal,* p. 2). Those who have argued for a strict morality have often covertly utilized a metaphysic which they have not felt compelled to justify (see John Wisdom, *Logic and Sexual Morality,* Penguin, Baltimore, 1965, pp. 68 ff. Hereafter: *Logic*). More commonly such arguments have been based on the easy transition between a change in our sexual ethics and the collapse of Western civilization or a similar catastrophe. Thus, as Reiss points out, there has been no substantial change in the American divorce rate since World War I, except for a brief post-World War II flurry (*Journal,* p. 126 f.). These breaches of proper intellectual discipline do not make it easy for those who favor a more liberal standard to find an open and thoughtful reception for their point of view. I do not want to minimize the genuine problems they still face in doing their research or promoting their ideas. I do, however, want to indicate what I think are some legitimate complaints against their logic. They do not always carefully observe the strictures they themselves lay down between science and ethics. Ira Reiss, regarded as one of the leaders in this field (Bell, *Premarital,* pp. 6, 64), whose careful statement on science and ethics was noted above, is a case in point.

Reiss does not hesitate to call the collection of articles he edited "The Sexual Renaissance in America," and he uses that term several times in his own contributions. It is doubtful whether there are objective sociological criteria for a "renaissance," and no effort is made to show how the term is scientifically derived from the material assembled. Further, he seems only to see possibilities of more permissive sex practices and never the possibility of reaction (p. 127). Thus Reiss is often less a scientist than a missionary. In the same volume Lester Kirkendall, in the article "Interpersonal Relationships—Crux of the Sexual Renaissance" (pp. 45 ff.), seems only to be reporting on a shift of sexual values, but it is difficult to avoid the impression that here, as in his book, he is urging us to accept a personalist ethical standard. I find this standard appealing but do not see how surveys on sex behavior can establish that any criterion should be accepted as the basis of our judgment of the rightness of sex acts.

The social scientist carries great weight in the American community today and even more in his classroom. He is, in general, an authority figure. But I am concerned lest the unthinking transfer his competence in gathering and sorting data to determining what men should or should not do. He may easily succumb to the temptation involved. There are methods of presenting data in an apparently impartial way which are, in effect, sly attacks upon old morals and subtle arguments for some other standard. As I do not want institutional religion to prevent open study and discussion of sex, so I do not want professors to bring moral pressures to bear on their students through abuse of authority gained in the field of science.

7. The relationship of what is to what ought to be done has been critical to modern discussions of ethics ever since G. E. Moore's work at the beginning of the century. If ethics has legitimacy as an autonomous realm of investigation and conclusion, then what is appropriate to its work must be consistent with the nature of that independent realm and not merely transferred from elsewhere. Thus, if what makes something potentially ethical stems from free self-determination, there is no logical entailment that the existence of any beings, such as God, or of any practice in society, such as opening doors for ladies, makes things "right" for me. That they exist may present certain practical problems, but this fact does not constitute an ethical obligation to conform to or rebel against them. They may, of course, present certain ethical possibilities to me, for I shall probably want to consider whether what people are doing or expect of me is what I really ought to do.

The critical ethical issue, then, is not the existence of a phenomenon or the widespread practice of an act but whether these commend themselves in the ethical realm. The question of what I believe to be right is most often understood in terms of an ideal or aspiration, of what is not often present and is only occasionally done. The ethical man wants to clarify this transcendent standard of conduct and apply it to the real situations of life.

What is usually at stake in arguments between behavioral scientists and ethicists is the relation of observations to standards. Men live in a world which we can usefully describe in mathematical, chemical, and other objective terms. If science could discover man's necessary nature basic to his behavior, there would be ethical implications. Such findings indicate what man has to be and hence take us from a realm where he is free to determine what he ought to be. For this reason, there has been much recent interest in the source of man's aggressiveness, i.e., whether it is necessary or not. (See, for example, the efforts of Herbert Marcuse to rework Freud's pessimism as expressed in *Civilization and Its Discontents,* in his book *Eros and Civilization*; see also Norman O. Brown, *Life Against Death,* and Erich Fromm, *The Heart of Man*; for a biological view, see Konrad Lorenz, *On Aggression,* and Robert Ardrey, *The Territorial Imperative*.) If man must make war, the real question is not whether it should be done but what kinds of war are compatible with that necessity. Thus, it would affect our sense of what is ethical in the sexual realm if we knew people had to have a certain number of satisfactory heterosexual orgasms to be happy and productive—information we do not yet possess.

Behind the reliance on psychology in John Wisdom's sexual ethics (see *Logic*) seems to lie the hope that science may yet reveal to us man's necessary sexual structure. After carefully describing the usefulness and limits of science in dealing with sexuality (pp. 37-47), he places his hope for a more satisfactory standard in what psychology has yet to teach us about human sexuality (pp. 44-45). Psychology can teach us a great deal about what people do sexually and what emotional effects this has upon them. But this only describes actual behavior and its consequences, not what our ideals ought to be. Most ethical deliberation assumes that man can come to be reasonably free in what he can do. This assumption leads beyond what he can do to a new and specifically ethical question: What should he do?

The intellectual difficulty arises when the behavioral scientist assumes or suggests that certain types of actual behavior indicate that a certain standard is unreasonable or another one is desirable. The logical question the ethicist asks is how one moves from what people do to what they ought to do. There may be reasons for such a deduction, but they are not given in the statistics themselves. The numbers simply report; they are not in themselves a mandate. They may be saying something about the limits of human freedom or the nature of man, but this remains a philosophical, not a statistical, issue. There is a minority which argues that statistics establish what is right. However, the proof for this claim cannot be found in more statistics but only in demonstrating, in ethical terms, why the claim is justified, perhaps by defining ethics so as to legitimate that standard.

It is conceivable that there may be no philosophical legitimacy to the notion of an ethical realm or to the fact of man's ethical pursuit (another "is-ought" fallacy). These, too, are not questions that can be decided by observation. It is possible for the empirical scientist to become an ethical thinker, but the two are separate fields with different methods. The data relevant in one area do not have similar relevance in the other.

8. Careful students of the topic therefore prefer to speak of "the ethics of Judaism," which is philosophically far more defensible. Yet this formulation, separating the universal—the ethics—from the particular—Judaism—automatically introduces an element of superior and inferior which has always plagued this type of philosophy of Judaism. The history of this thinking merits a comment.

When, after centuries of segregation from European life, Jews were permitted to enter general society, the need for a modern intellectual statement of the nature of Judaism became compelling. German philosophical idealism provided an easily adaptable framework for the presentation of what seemed central to Judaism. For the religious person, the Kantian emphasis on ethics as fundamental to man made it possible to argue that Jewish religious law was essentially a system of ethical duty which, through its observance, brought the individual and his community to a high standard of ethical living. By contrast, Christianity, which emphasized the inner act of faith over the outer works of duty, was necessarily less true to the fundamental ethical nature of man. In many forms (the early orthodoxy of Samson Raphael Hirsch, the philosophic clarity of Hermann Cohen, or the more experientially oriented reworking of Leo Baeck) this point of view served to explain why Judaism was a universal religion and as such was entitled to be respected by all men and to serve as a force for bettering general humanity as well as its own community. For secular thinkers, the ethics of Judaism became a substitute for belief in God and His commandments. The outstanding intellectual proponent of this position was Ahad Ha'am, the Zionist theoretician of the first part of this century. He was too much a positivist in the modern scientific sense to accept religion. Yet he was too deeply imbedded in the Jewish past to accept the notion that land and language alone could constitute the foundations of Jewish nationality. He insisted therefore that Jewish national character involved a personal and social commitment to ethics. Thus, roughly following Kant, he could have a purely secular ethics and use it to reinterpret Jewish religious literature and practice. That position, without Ahad Ha'am's profound sense of peoplehood, still moves many secular Jews today. They will talk of Jewish values, meaning largely its ethical passion, because they still want to be Jews but cannot accept Judaism's God or any concept of revelation.

Both positions suffer from the judgment implied in the standard of explanation they have adopted. The ethics justify Judaism, but because the latter is necessarily a particular, time-bound, and ethnically oriented expression of them, it is necessarily inferior to pure ethics. Hence Judaism is inevitably thrown on the defensive, and we are compelled to explain why we should bother about the nonethical elements in it. It is wonderful that Passover is a festival of human freedom, but why can't it be celebrated on a weekend when it is convenient? And how does eating bread during the festival lessen the impact of its meaning? It is valuable that the Jews used religion to make ethics a way of life before modern philosophy discovered it in its clarity, but now that it has been done, why do we need the old ways or the old group any longer? These are the sort of questions asked by the Jew who rationalizes his nonobservance by insisting that the Golden Rule is the heart of all religion.

This explanation of Judaism, for all the important insights it still retains, is obsolete. It was a brilliant construction for a day when most Jews still had deep religious roots. Then the problem was to direct Jews out into the larger human community. Today most Jews are citizens of the larger world, and the primary Jewish problem seems to be to determine what about them is still authentically Jewish. Once particularity has to be justified, the ethical approach fails. Is there a special Jewish ethics, or are there special ideas which Jews bring to bear on their ethical behavior? If so, it is extraordinary that in all the elaboration of this position there has been no major book on the ethics of Judaism since Hermann Cohen's *Religion of Reason,* written during World War I (if this work is ruled out as far too broad and unsystematic, we must retreat into the nineteenth century, to Moritz Lazarus). The reason would seem to be that such a book cannot be written either from the Jewish or the philosophic side. From the Jewish viewpoint, one must do violence either to the primacy of Jewish law, which was more than ethical, or insist that Jews alone can hold certain beliefs, as if ideas somehow can be confined or restricted to a few. Philosophically, the certainty which Kant brought to the reality and structure of the ethical in human life is no longer self-evident. Kant made the ethical the foundation of understanding man, history, and God. Today one of the major problems of modern thought is to see if value can be established and defined at all—and many philosophers have given up that hope. I therefore believe that any effort to interpret Judaism in modern terms cannot hope to prove Judaism's ethical superiority. Rather I think we must follow an existential tack by understanding man and his relation to God first and then legitimating the ethical as part of the religious. Hence I do not argue in this book from any special universal ethical wisdom that Judaism possessed in its teachings about and practice of human sexual relations. For purposes of communication, I am starting from the universal ground of what it means to be a person and bring to bear on our problem such general wisdom as my Jewish faith provides. (The relation of my own Jewish faith to a universal ethics is explicitly stated in the last chapter of this book and developed in greater detail in two of my other books, *A New Jewish Theology in the Making* and *What Can a Jew Say About Faith Today?*)

9. See the statement by the Group for the Advancement of Psychiatry, *Sex and the College Student,* Report No. 60, New York, 1965 (hereafter: GAP). It faces the various problems of late adolescent sexual experience in a sensitive and responsible way. Yet the permissiveness potentially involved in the Freudian or post-Freudian understanding of man is subtly affirmed: "Maturity of personality enhances the freedom both actively to enjoy sexuality and to choose and bear abstinence when it is necessary" (p. 110). Note that, while recognizing the alternatives available to freedom, it contrasts the positive "enjoy" of the one with the "bear" and "when it is necessary" of the other. The point is slight but indicative. The assumption is that sexual activity is always desirable, though the social context is left open. That such an attitude is in evidence even here explains a fortiori why,

among those who are less careful and far less responsible, Freud—generally unread and even more unheeded—becomes an excuse for urging more sexual activity of every sort.

10. GAP is helpful in outlining the range of problems involved. See especially pp. 24, 26-27, 33-37, 43.

11. I have not derived my judgment about high school students from the GAP report. Its authors would probably disparage any general judgment about a correlation of age with personal maturity. Many 16- and 17-year-olds are mature indeed. Yet after reading the GAP report, with its description of the psychological problems to be faced in late adolescence, particularly in this area, one is left wondering at what later stage of life most people are ready for responsible judgments concerning sex. I also find it interesting that, despite a cultural setting that demanded early responsibility, Jewish marriages over the centuries, as we shall see, were contracted in the late teen years.

12. The GAP report confines itself to "normal development and its ramification for the individual" (pp. 110-11). Yet it frequently makes reference to the ways in which even normal people use sexuality for other than directly sexual purposes (e.g., pp. 26 and 29). The problems are obviously far more formidable for the neurotic.

13. In a survey made of three hundred University of Wisconsin coeds by Halleck and Sternbach it was discovered, as noted above, that 22 percent of them had engaged in intercourse. When the figures were correlated with those who were receiving psychiatric treatment, they showed that 86 percent had had intercourse, and 72 percent of these with more than one person. The authors concluded that "permissive sexual activity seems to be highly correlated with mental illness" (*America*, June 10, 1967). No sound generalizations can be made from these statistics, yet they represent a reality which cannot be ignored. Sex offers one way of trying to escape from, or work out, personal problems, but becoming involved in sexual intercourse is also a way of precipitating them.

14. In formulating these four varieties of sexual ethics, I have given more weight to the philosophical problems involved in justifying each standard ethically than to any empirical evidence concerning what people think is right about having intercourse. The formal data on the thinking of college students in this area have been carefully gathered and summarized by Winston Ehrmann (*Premarital Dating Behavior*, Henry Holt and Co., New York, 1959), Lester Kirkendall (*Premarital Intercourse and Interpersonal Relationships*, Julian Press,

New York, 1961), and Ira Reiss (*Premarital Sexual Standards in America,* The Free Press of Glencoe, New York, 1960), who is explicitly concerned with elucidating standards. More informal insight into the thinking of college students today is given in *Sex and the College Girl,* by Gael Greene (Dell Publishing Co., New York, 1964), which despite its commercial sensationalism emerges as a serious, probing investigation into what young women are thinking. This empirical reality has considerable bearing on what I defined as the four types of standards. Otherwise they would have little to do with life. Nevertheless, for the sake of clarity, it seemed best to create types that proceeded from the reality of distinct ethical positions. Thus, the emphasis on freedom as fundamental to any ethical decision-making is stated under the influence of the Sartrean reworking of the Kantian sense of autonomy, though I have dissociated myself from that position because I consider it inadequate for ethics, and have attempted to formulate principles which would guide man's freedom. The ethics of healthy orgasm thus directs individual freedom in terms of a Freudian sense of normal, developmental, sexual activity. In an extreme form, it is reflected in the work of Wilhelm Reich.

The ethics of mutual consent is founded on a Kantian sense of respect for the will of another and the corollary insistence that a person must never be used as an end but only as a means. The ethics of love runs wide through the whole range of thinkers who expouse the so-called new morality. In its essence it is given the finest expression in Martin Buber's writings about the meaning of being a person and its relation to the proper kind of interpersonal dialogue. The ethics of marriage is presented in an existentialist interpretation of the traditional institution. It represents my view that institutions can have meaning for modern man only when they are explained in terms of their personal significance. At the same time I go beyond Buber in what I see to be his major limitation for an interpretation of Judaism, namely, his inability to authorize more than what the moment gives. Two hybrid proposals arise in the course of the argument: the ethics of consent based on a friendship, and that of an engaged couple. Since the former combines consent with love and the latter, love with marriage, they are discussed not as pure types but as progressions on a fixed scale. I have included a special note on applying pragmatic ethical standards, as Wisdom does (see below, note 16).

15. For a good introduction to Freud's sense of the sexual and the way it ultimately comes to concentrate itself in the genital stage, see

Norman O. Brown, *Life Against Death,* Wesleyan University Press, Conn., 1959, Chaps. III and IV. As to why Freud could find no satisfactory solutions to the human situation if that development were accepted as natural and necessary, see Part Four, "Sublimation." The "heresy" of Wilhelm Reich was precisely that he came to believe that full-scale genital expression of the libido would lead to health and creativity. See Reich's *Function of the Orgasm,* Orgone Institute Press, New York, 1948, and the comments on Reich by Brown, *op. cit.,* pp. 140-41.

16. John Wisdom is most compelling on this point. See his discussion of discrimination in action (*Logic,* p. 60), and its continuation through his attack on the belief that everything requires meaning to be worthwhile (p. 64). His emphasis on the virtue of desire and its satisfaction as the basis for search and experiment runs through the entire book. He makes several interesting suggestions for possible experimentation in the area of sexual activity. Yet it is not clear what one ought to do except continue the experiments. Search and understanding become ends in themselves. What one is looking for in the search is not clearly defined. Are all desires to be acted on? What does it mean to satisfy a desire, or when is a desire satisfactorily fulfilled? If sexual experiment is valid only because it is experiment, then not only are we without any substantive guide to our activity but the only real goal in sex becomes novelty. Novelty may be a helpful antidote to the assumption that one already knows all truth. Yet there is a compulsive dissatisfaction built into this attitude which may lead to despair. Wisdom is not unaware of human realities. Yet he has a strong faith in human desire and reason leading to the right. He seems to assume that every reasonable man will agree that there are certain limits beyond which one should not go. This is a kind of gentlemen's agreement about what "just isn't done" that is often made in the philosophic community so that it will not have to set any limits to the empirical method it advocates. When Wisdom does speak of substantive rather than methodological considerations, he does so in terms of what it means to be a person (see, e.g., p. 90). I, too, believe we must be open to the possibility of more satisfactory forms for our sexual life than we may have experienced, but I am equally, if not more, concerned with the problem of how to be a person in our civilization. Experimentation ought to be directed toward that end. I do not see it as a good in itself. I believe that there are real limits to experimentation, though they are often difficult to define and we have long erred in defining them too strictly. In any case, since the pragmatic method either advo-

cates what is already contained in the freedom precondition or—when it moves beyond it—will reasonably accept one of the four stated criteria of fulfillment/satisfaction, I have given it no additional consideration in this work.

17. Rather than footnote each author mentioned in this chapter as representative of a particular position, I have listed their relevant works in the bibliography.

18. This is precisely the assumption which Paul Ramsey argues cannot be granted. (See "A Christian Approach to Sexual Relations," *The Journal of Religion,* Vol. XLV, 1965, pp. 100-118.) He insists that sexual intercourse, as Christianity understands it, is inseparably linked by God with procreation. This bond does not emerge from a biological reality which can be altered by modern chemistry, but represents a deeply human reality which affects the meaning of the act. Only as a practical concomitant of this definition does he then argue that all methods of contraception involve some risk, thus assigning to procreation a practical as well as a theological dimension in intercourse. He further feels that married intercourse with contraception is procreative in the broader sense he is using and, thus, acceptable to God. Yet without the marriage bond intercourse cannot be procreative and hence is not justified. He is also careful to interpret marriage in human, and not ceremonial or legal, terms.

The Jewish tradition did not claim to know God's purposes; it concentrated on His commandments. It knew the command to procreate and took it seriously. However, in some cases in which God's purpose is clear (as in the pain accompanying childbirth) the tradition moves in an opposite direction. There is never a question in rabbinic literature about the propriety of using anesthetics. (See Immanuel Jakobovits, *Jewish Medical Ethics,* Bloch Publishing Co., New York, 1959, p. 104.) Here concern for the person has overridden the specific statement of the biblical text. However, the same process has not yet taken place in traditional Jewish law with regard to contraception, even though the position of Jewish tradition is far more liberal than that of the Roman Catholic church. See the clear and thorough discussion of the development of Jewish law on this topic by David Feldman, *Birth Control In Jewish Law* (New York University Press, 1968; hereafter: *Birth Control*).

19. GAP, pp. 43, 50 ff.

20. *Ibid.,* pp. 50-51.

21. *Ibid.,* p. 52; see also pp. 106-7.

22. The relevant data are summarized by Immanuel Jakobovits, *Jewish Medical Ethics,* Bloch Publishing Co., New York, 1959, Chap. 14, and more specifically, p. 183. David Feldman's discussion is particularly interesting not only for its delineation of the development of Jewish law in this area but for its careful contrast with Christian teaching (*Birth Control,* Chaps. 14 and 15).

23. P. 51.

24. See the discussion of the current literature and argumentation in Robert H. Springer, S.J., "Notes on Moral Theology: July-December, 1966," *Theological Studies,* Vol. 28, No. 2, June 1967, pp. 326-27.

25. My position, however, stems from a different standard of judgment than the one given in the following argument: "Contraception is unnatural, and men should not violate what is nature's law. Contraception introduces an artificial element into sexual relations and thus is a means of family planning which violates the natural order." The difficulty with this type of judgment is that it does not define what is "natural" and whether, ultimately, it is not man's nature to transform nature. It seems clear that we are ethically free to remedy the physical ills of mankind, such as headaches or infantile paralysis, and that we may improve upon the functioning of nature, as with vitamins or fluorides. Thus, one might argue that contraception is another means by which man helps nature do better what it intended but now does imperfectly. Since what distinguishes man from all other creatures is his ability to transform nature from its impersonal and even indifferent ways to patterns that are more congenial to his ends, contraception is merely one of the acts by which man, in accord with his nature, adapts impersonal nature to his volitional style instead of remaining constrained by its deterministic regularity. Obviously, I see sexual intercourse not in terms of natural law but in terms of personal relationships. The advocates of natural law are deeply concerned with persons, too, but believe that the full person comes into being only in conformity to the ethical patterns inherent in nature. The personalists argue that this position actually subordinates personal reality to impersonal standards. They see their opponents making the nature of the act itself more important than its effects on the lives of the people involved. Yet how can the fact that the child is naturally conceived supersede the fact that it is personally unwanted? The naturalists maintain that people should learn to accept and grow with the natural consequences of their actions. The personalists maintain that people ought to use every appropriate means to conform nature to their

responsible human ends, of which intercourse without children is one.

This controversy over values can be illustrated by pointing out how, for each of these two views, contraception shapes the meaning of intercourse for the partners involved. The advocates of natural law say that the employment of any contraceptive technique necessarily makes the act of intercourse less full and freely giving than it would be if it were natural. Like the naturalist, I affirm the legitimacy of intercourse as an expression of love and not solely as a means for the conception of children. However, the full giving of the self, one to the other, in the act will be conditioned by the knowledge that a child will not be conceived unless wanted. The rhythm method involves needless risk. Contraceptives offer reasonable security. The issue is not simply psychological tension or personal anxiety but, rather, a fundamental sense of ethical value. I believe using an abstract pattern of impersonal nature as the criterion of decision for a highly personal act is contrary to legitimate human self-determination. Since I am concerned primarily with personal, not natural, values, I consider the rhythm method of birth control, even for married people, of considerably less ethical value than mechanical or chemical means of contraception. According to Feldman, who cites abundant evidence, reliability is a major factor in determining what contraceptives Jews may legally use, though only in relation to the married (see *Birth Control,* p. 247, for the context).

26. The GAP report prefers to speak of adolescent idealism as an immature form of adjustment to reality. Much of what it says illuminates the responsibility of parents and others who deal with young people. See pp. 45-46.

27. The presentation here in the area of sex relations makes no claim to completeness. A good basic introduction to the data can be found in the work of Louis Epstein. Of particular value is his book *Sex Laws and Customs in Judaism,* Bloch Publishing Co., New York, 1948 (hereafter: *SLC*), and his article "The Institution of Concubinage Among the Jews," *Proceedings of the American Academy of Jewish Research,* Vol. 6, 1934-35, pp. 153-88 (hereafter: *Concubinage*). Of interest too is his volume *The Jewish Marriage Contract,* Jewish Theological Seminary of America, New York, 1927 (hereafter: *JMC*). His work, however, is marked by an apologetic tendency that should be balanced by a fresh look at the sources cited as well as their supplementation by other data and interpretations. Nevertheless, without Epstein's contribution it would be difficult for the nonspecialist in the history of Jewish law to make his way into this realm.

Another helpful volume, though it deals primarily with the legalities of betrothal and marriage rather than with premarital sexual problems, is Abraham Freiman, *Sefer Kidushin Venisuin,* Mosad Harav Kuk, Jerusalem, 1945 (hereafter: *Sefer*). Of special relevance is the brief section on what he calls *zivugim hofshiyim,* pp. 355-61.

Using their work as a starting point, I have tried to bring together all significant data relevant to Jewish attitudes and practice which I could find. To give the reader something of the tone of traditional reasoning, I have freely paraphrased a number of documents, sacrificing textual accuracy for immediately understood terms.

28. Exodus 21:10-11 speaks of a woman's marital rights (in this case a slave who had been bought for that purpose). These are food, clothing, and a third term which the rabbis generally interpret as sexual intercourse. She is entitled to have intercourse, and her husband owes it to her in addition to his personal responsibility to beget children. Both, then, are divine commandments which he must obey. Thus a woman, though she generally has few rights in this area, may demand a divorce if her husband refuses to have intercourse with her. The Mishnah records the following limits even to his making a religious vow (something of great seriousness to the rabbis): "If a man took a vow not to have intercourse with his wife, the School of Shammai says she may consent and thus make it effective, but only for a period of two weeks. The School of Hillel says she may consent to such a vow only for a period of one week" (Ket. 5:6). See the comments of Epstein, *JMC,* p. 218, interpreting the discussion of the Talmud relative to this material. Should he make the vow for a longer period, the rabbinical court cannot force him to break the vow. Yet though the court cannot compel him to divorce for abstaining from intercourse, it can force a divorce for making such a vow! Feldman conclusively makes the point that one of the reasons Jewish law permitted contraception under certain circumstances was that it considered intercourse critical to the proper sort of married life. See *Birth Control,* Chaps. 3-5, and the careful delineation of the wife's rights and husband's needs as defined in Chap. 4 and referred to *passim.*

29. The Christian charge that Judaism is essentially legalism and that Pharisaism is necessarily a harsh and impersonal form of religiosity has often been refuted by Christian scholars knowledgeable in rabbinic literature, such as Herford, Moore, and presently, Davies, as well as by Jewish writers. Yet it still manages to appear occasionally, and not always in backward or unsophisticated persons. John Wisdom,

in several short sentences, dismisses the Jewish Bible as "the Old Testament level," inferior to the religion of love created by both the Buddha and Jesus and the level at which most of us are still unfortunately "stuck." Wisdom even insists that most societies of 600 B.C.E. "held an ideal not dissimilar from the notion of the Law as it appears in the Old Testament" (p. 93). It is not just the ignorance of the ancient Near East which is appalling but the willingness of a man who is fully committed ethically to openness in matters of sex to refuse to examine his old prejudices regarding biblical Judaism. The Jewish legalist has been called a religious behaviorist by Abraham Heschel, who analyzes that position in *God in Search of Man,* Jewish Publication Society, Philadelphia, 1956, pp. 320-35.

30. Nothing seems to excite the imagination of scholars so much as the refusal of the Bible to give a direct answer to a question they have. They probably feel divine revelation should contain all the answers men require. Yet even when they do not accept the theory that the words are God's own, they seem to feel human imagination must compensate for the lack of data. Thus, Raphael Patai *(Sex and Family in the Bible and the Middle East,* Doubleday, Garden City, N.Y., 1959; hereafter: *Family)* argues for the existence of a strong sense of sexuality among the people of biblical times without giving any direct evidence for it but referring back from the rather romantic reports of nineteenth-century European travelers (pp. 163-65). By seizing on a biblical phrase or word, he seeks to construct an entire ethical theory. For example, he argues from Genesis 2:24, which says that a man and his wife shall become one flesh, that intercourse always renders one partially a kinsman and that for this reason incest is forbidden so strictly (pp. 157-58). David Mace *(Hebrew Marriage,* Epworth Press, London, 1953), who does not hesitate to use much later data to explain early marriage customs (p. 143), can argue that biblical sexual morality is related directly to the religious symbolism of the circumcised penis (an idea which, as far as I know, does not occur in Jewish sources until medieval mystic sources; p. 22 f.). He amalgamates the Exodus and Deuteronomy laws to give one general law which may "be regarded as covering all possible circumstances by which the man secures connexion with the girl . . ." (p. 228) and then gives a summary apologizing for the fact that the Bible does not regard premarital intercourse in these laws as a "moral" evil, though this sense is gradually dawning (pp. 239-40).

The truth of the matter is that we do not have much evidence or law on sexual relations, betrothal, or marriage in biblical times. Most of what we do have comes from Patriarchal times, which are not a good basis for arguing about the postsettlement period, or from our glimpses of the royal court during the single monarchy, another highly specialized source of insight. Consequently, Roland de Vaux (*Ancient Israel*, McGraw-Hill, New York, 1961; hereafter: *Israel*) sounds appealing when he says about marriage, "The Bible gives us no information about the age at which girls were married" (p. 29, and see the context from p. 26); or, on betrothal, "The historical books provide little information" (p. 32). And he can therefore say forthrightly about fornication what most biblical ethicists try to find ways of avoiding: "We have no information about unmarried women, except that a priest's daughter who turned to prostitution was to be burned alive" (p. 37; the last phrase is a non sequitur, since we have other data on prostitution, which is not identical with fornication).

31. Compare the perceptive discussion by Gerhard von Rad, *Old Testament Theology* (Harper and Row, New York, 1962 and 1966, 2 vols.), Vol. I, pp. 27-28, Vol. II, pp. 340, 349; hereafter: *Theology*.

32. Gen. 1:28.

33. Any biblical encyclopedia will provide the data concerning virginity in the Bible. An excellent summary with a rounded bibliography stressing cognate sources is to be found in *Entziklopedyah Mikrait*, Mosad Bialik, Jerusalem, Vol. 2, 1954, article "betulah," cols. 381-84. On the annual bewailing of Jepthah's daughter, see Judg. 11:40.

34. Deut. 22:13-21.

35. That there is a general conscience was taken for granted by Jewish tradition and recognized by Jewish law, though on occasion it became necessary to make explicit a command of conscience which had hitherto been assumed. Thus, no specific biblical law requires a man to support his wife or daughter, yet the rabbis, when they had to, could find ways of deriving these responsibilities from the Bible, even if indirectly. See Epstein, *JMC*, pp. 150, 286. For a general discussion of the problem, see Isaac Heinemann, *Taamei Hamitzvot*, The Jewish Agency, Vol. 1, 1959, p. 16. While this may well accord with Heinemann's interest in stressing the ethical aspect of the law, it is no violation of the tradition which could speak of laws such as incest as being known by logic even if they had not been given by revelation. We may reasonably say that the same applies to prostitution, since there is so much indirect evidence pointing in that direction. Yet I would

not apply this type of argument to premarital intercourse, where there is considerable legal and moral silence.

36. Niddah 5:7-8. Because it is neither clear when the title "Rabbi" emerged nor which man held what title in a given period, it has become conventional to put the sign "R." before everyone's name and read it as "rabbi."

37. Failure to distinguish between these stages can result in misunderstandings of the rabbis' comments. In Hebrew one can see which legal category is involved. In English one often cannot tell what the implication is. Here, for example, is a translation of a Gaonic document of the ninth century given by Z. W. Falk, in *Jewish Matrimonial Law in the Middle Ages,* Oxford University Press, London, 1966 (hereafter: *Matrimonial*): "He who despoils a maiden without a marriage contract and betrothal is liable to divine retribution. He commits an enormity. He may well bring a deluge on the world and delay the advent of the Messiah" (p. 93). This appears to be the earliest straightforward prohibition of premartial intercourse in Jewish literature. Yet a check of the Hebrew reveals that what is translated as "maiden" is the word *tinoket,* "a minor," a pre-*naarah,* i.e., a girl under twelve. The previous phrase in the text also makes clear that this is a special case of intercourse not only with an underage girl but almost certainly one to whom the man is betrothed.

38. For a good survey of the relevant material see section 2 of the article "Majority" in *The Jewish Encyclopedia,* Vol. 8, pp. 270-71 (reprinted by Ktav Publishing House Inc., New York; hereafter quoted only by title). Bernard Bamberger is especially concerned with the original reasons for the distinctions. See his thoughtful analysis in "Qetanah, Na'arah, Bogereth," in *Hebrew Union College Annual,* Vol. XXXII, Cincinnati, 1961, pp. 281-94. For some of the special rights to which the *naarah* was entitled under given circumstances, see Boaz Cohen, *Jewish and Roman Law,* Jewish Theological Seminary of America, New York, 1966, p. 298, note 94 (hereafter: *Roman*).

39. It is also reasonably certain that most girls never exercised such a privilege, as is evident from the comment of a tenth- or eleventh-century authority: "It is the custom of all Jewish girls who, though dwelling in their father's house, are mature (*bogeret*) or even twenty years old, to let their fathers arrange their marriages. They are not so immoral or so impudent as to express their own desires and say 'I want to marry so and so.'" Quoted in Israel Abrahams, *Jewish Life in the*

Middle Ages, Jewish Publication Society, Philadelphia, 1896, p. 166 (hereafter: *Life*).

40. For the specific legal forms see Freiman, *Sefer,* pp. 10-14. Rav is the major authority against giving one's daughter in marriage while she is yet a minor and before she is a *naarah* (Kid. 41a-b). On the other hand, as we shall see, marriage delayed until a girl was over twelve and a half was also discouraged (San. 76a-b). For boys the late teens seem to be the most desired time. One fanciful account says that in the good old days Jews used to marry their sons at 12 and their grandsons at 12, so that at 26 a man was already a grandfather (Lam. Rab. 1:1, para. 2). The various opinions recorded in Kid. 29b-30a seem far more realistic. Several set 20 as the top limit for marriage for a male (thus, too, *Pirke Avot* 5:21). Others give ranges from 16 to 22 or 18 to 24. The reason given for the early marriage is stated explicitly by R. Hisda, who traced his preeminence over his colleagues to his marriage at 16. Yet had he married at 14, he noted, he could have completely defeated the evil urge. So, too, R. Huna contends that he who is not married at 20 spends all his days in sin or, as the comment follows, really in sinful thoughts. Hayyim Schauss asserts that marriages were sometimes delayed until the age of 30 or 40 because of the many wars in this period but his sources do not bear this out (*The Lifetime of a Jew,* Union of American Hebrew Congregations, Cincinnati, 1950, p. 148, note 162; hereafter: *Lifetime*).

41. The rabbis apparently believed that at the time a girl becomes a *bogeret* the signs of her virginity naturally decrease. Thereafter it would be difficult to apply the normal standards to her. Hence they rule that one who marries a *bogeret* may not raise a question about her virginity. This may be connected with their general rulings that the laws concerning the penalties for rape or seduction do not apply in the case of a nonvirgin. See Epstein, *JMC,* p. 72, on that account and, in general, the article "bogeret" in *Entziklopedyah Talmudit,* Jerusalem, Vol. 2, 1956, pp. 377-79; hereafter: *En. Tal.*

42. San. 76a-b.

43. There are some isolated data from Hellenistic literature. Ben Sirach, in the Apocrypha, written probably in the last part of the third century B.C.E., speaks of the importance of marrying one's daughter to an intelligent man (7:25), of having a good wife (26:1-3), and the undesirability of being a bachelor (36:24-26). The second book of Maccabees refers to the practice of keeping young girls secluded. Describing a riot, the author says, "the maidens, who were kept indoors, ran to-

gether, some to the walls, and some looked out from the windows . . ."
(II Macc. 3:19). Philo of Alexandria, in a long discussion of Jewish law,
writes, "The corruption of a maiden is a criminal offense, closely akin
to adultery, its brother in fact, for both spring, as it were, from one
mother, licentiousness. . . ." He is not speaking here of an engaged
girl or even of one who might come under the laws of seduction or
rape, as the following pages make clear. He refuses to justify nonmarital intercourse on the grounds of love but insists it can only be
right within the context of marriage (*The Special Laws,* III, XI, 65,
pp. 515-16, Loeb Classical Library, Harvard University Press, Cambridge, Mass.). Samuel Belkin calls Philo "the harshest Jewish writer"
on this topic (*Philo and the Oral Law,* Harvard University Press, Cambridge, Mass., 1940, p. 245).

44. Two classic citations from the literature of the period following the early crusades are worth quoting: "The custom that prevails
among us of marrying off our daughters even while they are still minors
results from the daily increase of our sufferings in exile. Though today
a man may be able to afford a dowry for his daughter, he may by to-
morrow be unable to give her anything and she may remain unmarried
forever" (Tos. Kid. 41a). The other is ascribed to Perez ben Elijah of
Corbeil (d. ca. 1295): "The Talmudic prohibition of child marriages
applied only to the period when many Jewish families were in the
same town. Now, however [after the crusades], when our numbers are
reduced and our people are scattered we are in the habit of marrying
girls under the age of twelve, should an eligible husband present himself" (as quoted by Israel Abrahams, *Life,* pp. 169-70, and see the
sources given there). These remarks explain why at about that time
what had earlier been two ceremonies, with the contract written at the
former, became one ceremony preceded by agreement on the match,
with the contract now written at the later, combined event (see Epstein, *JMC,* pp. 13-16). Jacob Katz says that the normal age for marriages in the period 1500-1750 was about sixteen for girls and eighteen
for boys, though earlier marriages were encouraged and some took
place later (see Jacob Katz, *Tradition and Crisis,* Free Press, Glencoe,
Ill., 1961, p. 139; hereafter: *Tradition.* But see also p. 142, where
class factors are noted. For the relevant source materials, consult the
Hebrew edition, *Masoret Umishbar,* Mosad Bialik, Jerusalem, 1958.)
Abrahams points out that a special problem arose in the second half of
the seventeenth century, when child marriages became quite common
under the influence of Sabbetai Zevi, whose mystic theories involved an

attempt to bring all the souls created in heaven into being on earth so that the time of the Messiah's coming would have arrived (*Life,* p. 168). Salo Baron notes numerous communal enactments designed to prevent such child marriages and postpone the ceremony to the later teen years, but these did not always receive ready compliance (*The Jewish Community,* Jewish Publication Society, Philadelphia, 1942, Vol. II, pp. 310-11; hereafter: *Community*).

45. The relevant data are summarized in Cohen, *Roman,* p. 321, especially note 228 and the comparison with the Roman sense of betrothal. Abraham Freiman says that to the end of the first millennium the period between bethrothal and marriage was long. Many apparently found it too long; hence there are many Gaonic warnings against intercourse between the betrothed (*Sefer,* p. 17).

46. See the pertinent remarks by Salo Baron, *A Social and Religious History of the Jews,* Jewish Publication Society, Philadelphia, 1952, Vol. II, p. 219; hereafter: *History*.

47. San. 75a. There is a passage which bars a father from giving his daughter for intercourse to any man lacking the intent to marry her (see San. 76a). There the verse, "Do not profane your daughter to cause her to be a whore," interprets "whoring" as referring to any sexual immorality.

The rabbis seem to have thought exclusively of the chastity of the woman with regard to premarital intercourse. Although they expressed general surprise that one could learn genuine religiosity from a young girl, they cite with high commendation the case of a young woman who prayed that no man might fall into sin through her (Sotah 22a). If she were to allow herself to be seduced, her lover must pay her father in consideration, among other things, of the "blemish" which has now come on the family name, thus giving some legal status to the moral judgment (see Epstein, *SLC,* pp. 186 ff.). Her action has not only affected her and her family's name (a matter that recurs in medieval legal literature), but if she was betrothed at the time, it has really disparaged all the girls in Israel (Sifre to Deut. 22:21). Male chastity was also commended. See the famous comment of R. Johanan: "God proclaims the virtue of three people every day, the first of whom is a bachelor who lives in a large town without sinning . . ." (Pes. 113a-b). There is also a tradition of high praise for Joseph, who resisted Potiphar's wife, and it stresses his sexual self-mastery as well as his concern for her status as a married woman and non-Jewess. See Louis Ginzberg,

The Legends of the Jews, Jewish Publication Society, Philadelphia, 1925, Vol. V, pp. 324-25.

There are some rabbinic references to the reality of sexual immorality among the unmarried. In several halachic discussions the rabbis make reference to loose women who might be expected to give in to sexual temptation, and they recognize that the law needed to be construed so as not to give them any opportunity to do so (e.g., Ket. 3b).

At least two passages seem to show a more tolerant view of male promiscuity, one of them undoubtedly referring to prostitution: "R. Hisda said, 'Immorality in a house is like a worm in a sesame plant,' . . . but that is said in reference to a woman and not in reference to a man" (Sotah 3b. There is a typical apologetic rejoinder in the Soncino translation, p. 11, note 2. *The Babylonian Talmud,* ed. Isidore Epstein, The Soncino Press, London, 1936). Another passage reports that "R. Ilai said, 'If a man should find that his evil inclination is overpowering him, let him go to a place where no one knows him, dress himself entirely in black, and do as his heart desires, but let him not profane the name of God in public.' Is this teaching not a contradiction to the one which states that he who does not show concern for the honor of his Creator had better not have been born? That saying was interpreted by R. Joseph as referring to a man who sins in secret! There is no contradiction between them. In the first case we are talking about a man who cannot control his desires, but in the second case we are talking about a man who could have controlled them yet gave in to them in secret" (Kid. 40a). I do not think that we have a standoff between these two positions, with the rabbis taking a neutral stand equidistant from both extremes. The very insistence of the anonymous response to R. Ilai's suggestion and even the solution offered to it indicate that granting even so modest a permission as a visit to a prostitute offended the general rabbinic sensibility. When these passages are put in the context of other opinions and the laws the rabbis created to separate men from women, it seems clear where the overwhelming weight of their opinion lay. These two passages are then best seen as exceptional concessions to reality rather than as a statement of their authors' or the rabbis' general ideal.

48. There seem to have been remarkably few Jewish prostitutes in biblical and rabbinic times. In neither period do we hear of Jews who own or operate houses of prostitution. When Jews became involved with prostitutes, they were generally pagan women.

The relative paucity of Jewish prostitutes remained a reality until
the end of ghetto segregation. Since that time there is some evidence
that prostitution has become measurable among Jews as part of the
breakdown in morals that marks their transition to the modern world.
On the historical background, see Epstein, *SLC,* pp. 163-67, and particularly notes 58, 59, and 63.

There is great leniency toward the prostitute herself under Jewish
law. Her children may carry a certain moral stigma, but they are not
technically illegitimate under Jewish law, or *mamzerim,* for these are
only the offspring of adulterous relations. Violating the marriage covenant was more serious to Jewish law than being a prostitute. The
best summary of Jewish law on this topic is, as usual, *En. Tal.,* Vol. 12,
article "zonah," pp. 49-74. The article limits itself severely, as always,
to recounting the legal issues and the relevant data and does not
branch out into more general ethical or historical issues.

49. The rabbis are rarely unanimous on a topic, as they are, for
example, by their stand against idolatry. And even where they are, they
often differ substantially on exactly what their thinking implies for
action. On most matters there seems to be a broad spectrum of opinion,
with individual sages, on occasion, apparently contradicting themselves.
None of these positions would appear to have more authority than
the others. Their personal and historical contexts are generally unknown to us. Sometimes we can only conclude that there is no such
central view. Hence it is frequently difficult to determine what may be
called normative Judaism.

The rabbis tended to think in terms of cases, stories, or contexts,
where we think in abstract concepts. When we try to impose our ab-
stractions upon their way of thinking and its records, we find ourselves making little contact. In order to understand them and their
particular stance in their own context, we must find the terms, concepts, and categories which they used that most closely correspond to
our question.

It seems clear that the rabbis do not think in terms of "premarital
intercourse" or "fornication." The modern Hebrew equivalents for
these terms are not helpful for research in rabbinic literature. In practice, there is more to be learned of the rabbis' attitudes to sex ethics
from their discussions of "concubines" or "the mature young woman,"
than from those dealing with "intercourse."

50. The words customarily used by the rabbis in this context all
derive from the root z-n-h. In the Bible, *zonah,* when used as a noun,

means "prostitute" in quite the same sense that the term is used today. It is also used as a verb to describe intercourse as part of pagan religious activity or as the commission of an adulterous act. By extension it comes to mean acting falsely against God and takes on similar metaphorical uses. In the rabbinic literature the verb goes far beyond prostitution to include any immoral sexual act. (Comparable noun usages are also common.) Thus, the verb may refer specifically to visiting or being a prostitute. It may equally well refer to adultery or, since the legal state of adultery does not apply to males, to a husband's extramarital intercourse. It may refer to an act connected with sexuality, psychological or actual, of which the rabbis disapproved. Hence, one cannot simply apply rabbinic statements that use some form of the root *z-n-h* to the present topic without great care. The problem is further complicated by most English translations of rabbinic documents, which tend, under the influence of nineteenth-century prudery, to make the texts sound more ethical and spiritual, and less earthy and direct, than they are. For the occurrence of the root *z-n-h* in the Bible, see Brown, Driver, and Briggs, *Hebrew and English Lexicon of the Old Testament,* Oxford University Press, London, 1906, pp. 275-76; and in rabbinic literature, Marcus Jastrow, *Dictionary,* Title Publishing Co., New York, 1943, Vol. I, p. 406; Mosheh David Gross, *Otzar Haagadah,* Mosad Harav Kuk, Jerusalem, Vol. 2, 1961, entry "zenut," pp. 349-52; and the unpublished rabbinic thesis of H. Richard White, *Zenut and Peritzut in Aggadic Literature,* Hebrew Union College-Jewish Institute of Religion, New York, 1966.

Halachic usage seems to employ the term in a more general way. The Torah says that a priest may not marry a *zonah.* There are a number of rabbinic traditions that *zonah* in this context is not to be interpreted literally but refers to women in various categories, from a convert to anyone who had intercourse with a man she was not married to, with or without payment. Hence, much of their concern with intercourse as described by this term has to do with technical, not general moral, questions, such as: What sort of intercourse renders the woman a *zonah* for purposes of barring her from marrying anyone of a priestly family?

There is a second important legal usage of the term—the strong tradition that the act of intercourse itself once constituted a means of marrying a woman. The rabbis considered this tradition immoral and tried to end the practice (see note 83, below, for the relevant data). Yet great importance was attached to the general supposition *ein adam oseh beilato beilat zenut* ("a man who has intercourse with a woman he is eligible to marry must not be presumed to have done so as an act of *zenut*"; that is, his intention in intercourse must be assumed to be for purposes of marriage). However, unless that understanding was mitigated, every act of intercourse between two marriageable Jews would in effect create a marriage between them which in turn would require a divorce before they could marry others. Without a divorce, in any subsequent marriages the woman would transgress the laws of adultery, her children would be *mamzerim,* fully illegitimate, and the man, in later years when the prohibition of polygamy was in force, would contravene that ban. Hence the rabbis eventually restricted this principle virtually to a man's intercourse with his divorced wife or to specific cases where the intent to marry was made manifest (*En. Tal.,* Vol. 1, article "ein adam oseh beilato beilat zenut," pp. 257-61).

The general term for sexual immorality often carries legal overtones referring only to disqualification from priestly marriage or to the fact that such an act does not establish a marriage. The latter is particularly intriguing, since the rabbis are anxious to avoid even a presumption which will stand in the way of a later proper marriage and accordingly may prefer to say that the couple had *zenut* intercourse rather than marriage (e.g., Ket. 3a). One might infer that the rabbis do not take such intercourse very seriously. They may also give this impression in the former area when they argue that a single act of intercourse does not make a woman a *zonah,* as if somehow every woman were entitled to one adventure. Neither interpretation would be warranted. The rabbis are not making judgments here about *zenut* intercourse. Rather they are going far out of their way to defend the structure and make practical the observance of Jewish law concerning marriage. This purpose is so important to them that they are willing to expand certain categories of illicit intercourse and not attach censure to them (on this point see Falk, *Matrimonial,* pp. 33-34).

It is also possible to see this term *beilat zenut,* "*zenut* intercourse," as implying an ethical condemnation of the acts, since it seems derived from the term for general sexual immorality, *zenut.* Yet I question whether this connotation is appropriately read here or whether the rabbis used it as a technical, legal category, value-free, so to speak. They had no other term for it. A variety of translations of the term can illustrate the problem: "connexion of the nature of fornication" (Herbert Danby, *The Mishnah,* Oxford University Press, London,

1933, p. 227); "intercourse of the nature of prostitution" (Philip Blackman, *Mishnayoth,* The Judaica Press, New York, 1965, Vol. III, p. 60); "meretricious intercourse" (Isidore Epstein, tr., *The Babylonian Talmud,* The Soncino Press, London, 1936, Vol. Yevamoth, p. 409); "immoral intercourse" (Abraham Neuman, *The Jews in Spain,* Jewish Publication Society, Philadelphia, 1944, Vol. II, p. 41; hereafter: *Spain*). While the term is not completely neutral because of the general derogation of *zenut,* I believe it is less pejorative, when used in a legal context, than most of these translations would indicate. Otherwise it would not be possible to accommodate such opinions as that of R. Huna, who said that any intercourse which does not result in procreation is *beilat zenut.* (See Yev. 61b, the *locus classicus* on this topic.) In legal contexts I have therefore rendered it as "casual intercourse."

The other general rabbinic term for sexual immorality is *ervah.* Confined in the Bible to the usage of nakedness in regard to relatives (as specified in Lev. 18), it retains in rabbinic literature the primary meaning of "incest" but may extend to sexual immorality of a less familial nature (e.g., Sarah and Joseph in Egypt, Song of Sol. Rab., 4:12,1), or even to sights or sounds that might rouse one to sexual activity. Thus in statements using this term or others derived from it, one cannot make easy inference to the rabbinic attitudes toward premarital intercourse. Where incest is obviously not involved, it is difficult to know specifically what the rabbis had in mind. (See Jastrow, op. cit., Vol. II, pp. 1114 and 1115; Gross, op. cit., Vol. II, pp. 952-54; for the legal denotation only, *En. Tal.,* Vol. 1, article "gilui arayot," pp. 106-15).

As an example of the problem of euphemism, see the English rendering of the *takkanah,* the community enactment of Forli (p. 294). To modern ears the problem sounds quite premarital. The Hebrew text, however, after general alarms, gives some details, none premarital, but insists that it is not proper to say more. See Louis Finkelstein, *Jewish Self-Government in the Middle Ages,* Philipp Feldheim, Inc., New York, 1964, p. 286; hereafter: *Self-Government.*

51. The bulk of Louis Epstein's book *Sex Laws and Customs in Judaism* is devoted to this topic of indirect controls. For specific details and the relevant source materials, see Chap. II, "Modesty in Dress," Chap. III, "Sex Segregation in Public Places," and Chap. VI, "Purity of Mind." As we shall see later, one of the controls designed to prevent an unmarried man and woman from being alone together is

used by some authorities in the Middle Ages as a basis for outlawing nonmarital intercourse, even though they cannot find a biblical basis for their injunction.

52. Gen. Rabbah 9:7. For a general discussion of the rabbinic view, see the somewhat apologetic presentation by Solomon Schechter, *Aspects of Rabbinic Theology,* Schocken Books, New York, 1961, Chap. XV, "The Evil Yezer"; and George Foot Moore, *Judaism,* Harvard University Press, Cambridge, Mass., 1932, Part III, Chap. III, "The Origin of Sin." For a modern statement of the topic, together with some rabbinic materials interpreted in Freudian terms, see Arnold J. Wolf, "Psychoanalysis and the Temperaments of Man," in *Rediscovering Judaism,* Arnold J. Wolf, ed., Quadrangle Books, Chicago, 1965.

53. *Hil. Ishut,* Introduction and 1:4.

54. Rafael Patai argues on the basis of one usage of the term in the Judah and Tamar story that there is little difference between the *kedeshah* and the *zonah,* the ordinary prostitute. I find the argument unconvincing (*Family,* p. 150). See rather Roland de Vaux, *Israel,* p. 384, and Gerhard von Rad, *Theology,* Vol. I, p. 22, which also gives the general cultural context.

55. Epstein, *SLC,* p. 136, summarizes the relevant data.

56. See above, note 50, for the discussion of the complications concerning the term *zonah* in rabbinic law.

57. De Vaux, *Israel,* pp. 24-26. Several scholars, on the basis of rabbinic traditions about the *pilegesh,* argue that there was once a regular practice of buying Hebrew bondwomen for wives. The later rabbinic legislation making her a full wife is an effort to do away with this servant-*pilegesh.* The intent of the biblical purchase and the rabbinic legislation is clear, but I do not see the direct connection with the *pilegesh* in biblical times. The term is not used in connection with the slave legislation of Exod. 21, though there are obvious similarities between this situation and that of the concubine. See, for example, Boaz Cohen, *Roman,* pp. 329-35, and the attendant data cited there. See also Epstein, *JMC,* p. 9 and note 29. In any case, this historical aspect of the discussion is almost entirely irrelevant to the legal situation in the Middle Ages, with which we are concerned.

58. Epstein states that Josephus denies the practice of concubinage in his day, but he gives no source (*JMC,* p. 123). However, the data in rabbinic literature as well as the absence of actual cases provide an adequate basis for the statement.

59. The two major passages are Yer. Ket. 29d and the one I give in

English in the body of the text (San. 21a). The former contains R. Meir's opinion that a *pilegesh* differs from a wife only in not having a formal contract. R. Judah differs with him. The matter becomes more complicated and probably the basis of the Spanish practices (of which more below) when Rashi, in his comment to Gen. 25:6, cites the Sanhedrin passage and says merely that the *pilegesh* has no contract. Rav, however, had not simply agreed with R. Meir but had explicitly added that she also was not taken by any marriage rites. By omitting this fact, Rashi made possible the understanding that the *pilegesh* got her status by marriage rites or some sort of betrothal, though there was no binding contract. This accordingly gave rise to the later problems of the betrothed and free *pilegesh*. See the summary by Epstein, *JMC,* p. 10, note 31.

60. San. 21a.

61. Hil. Mel. 4:4.

62. Thus, in *The Guide of the Perplexed* he speaks of the bestial things related to touch, which is the foulest of the senses (II, 36), and then, citing Aristotle as the source of his judgment, goes on to speak of the act related most closely to it as "the foulness of copulation" (II, 40, p. 384, tr. Shlomo Pines, University of Chicago Press, 1963). The survey given by Epstein, *SLC,* pp. 20-22, regarding the general denigration of intercourse by the philosophers and moralists of this period, seems entirely reasonable.

63. Falk gives the Roman and the Christian background to the practice of concubinage, indicating that, while monogamy had become general by the ninth century, concubinage had also become more widely practiced (*Matrimonial,* pp. 22-24). Epstein also traces the non-Jewish backgrounds of concubinage and attributes its return among Jews to the influence of their non-Jewish environment (*Concubinage,* pp. 178-80). Almost all of the historical evidence is taken from the legal *responsa* on the topic. (Some data are available in sermons and apologetic works.) The opinions of some major historians on the problems of sexual practice in the Jewish community for several centuries beginning roughly with the twelfth century will be of interest.

The focus of critical concern is Spanish Jewry. Abraham A. Neuman distinguishes between two types of concubine, the one, formally betrothed by her lover, the other, freely taken by agreement. These are traced back in theory to the time of the Talmud, when, as Neuman agrees, the practice did not exist (*Spain,* Vol. II, pp. 37-39). In Spain, however, concubinage was practiced. What troubled the Jewish authorities, he feels, was the betrothed type (apparently because of the difficulties this involved with Jewish marriage law; on these legal matters, see the discussion of the actual documents themselves below in notes 67, 68, 70, and 71). "Emphatically, the concubine, who was a mistress living in unsanctified cohabitation, constituted no problem. Only a few instances of such relationships occur in the responsa and these were summarily repressed by the communal authorities as soon as they became known" (p. 39). "In the last resort, concubinage was a modified form of polygamy and existed only in those provinces where the latter was tolerated. . . . It justified itself in the popular mind as being less aggravating than the state of polygamy . . ." (p. 41). How widespread the practice was may be judged from the fact that of the 4500 *responsa* of Solomon ben Abret, Asher ben Yehiel, and his son Jacob which Neuman studied and classified, only five refer to the *pilegesh,* while eight deal with problems of adultery or other forms of illegal intercourse (*Spain,* p. 278, note 22). The evidence seems to imply that, while the problem was present and disturbing—particularly because, as we shall see, it lasted over a period of generations—it did not dominate the community or disturb its essential concern with marriage.

What apparently kept such sexual arrangements within bounds was the right of the officials of the Jewish community to take action for its general welfare, whether in terms of Jewish law or in order to preserve a pattern of life that would be acceptable to the non-Jews, among whom the Jews were a tolerated minority. The community court had a tradition of having its origin in the need to guard against the harlotry which leads to idolatry (San. 35a). It derived its broad powers from the precedent given in the Talmud (San. 46a). As interpreted by the rabbis, it gave the judges outside the land of Israel far more latitude than the courts of the classic rabbinic period had known. The later summary of their power in the *Shulhan Arukh, Hoshen Mishpat,* 2:425, and commentaries *ad loc.* give it almost unlimited power. See also the description of its functioning by Salo Baron, *Community,* Vol. II, pp. 216 ff. For an abstract description of the penalties the courts might use, see George Horowitz, *The Spirit of Jewish Law,* Central Book Co., N.Y., 1963, pp. 215-30. He says fornication and prostitution were generally punished by banishment, but he gives no source for this judgment (p. 226).

In Spain the community had an unusual way of carrying out this function. In some places there were officials called *berurei averot,* "investigators of vice," whose essential concern was almost certainly with sexual indiscretions. These took place not only within the Jewish community but between Jews and non-Jews, and were obviously a most important community concern (Yitzhak Baer, *A History of the Jews in Christian Spain,* Jewish Publication Society, Philadelphia, 1966, Vol. II, p. 66; and see also Vol. I, p. 225). However, it is Baer's opinion that the most prevalent sexual problem was prostitution, and not concubinage (Vol. II, p. 466, note 23). Isaiah Tishby ascribes the Zohar's continuing polemic against sexual relations with non-Jews to the practices of the Jews in its author's, Moses de Leon's, time (the end of the thirteenth century in Toledo). He argues that the major sexual sins of the day were not those which occasionally arose between Jews but rather the many relationships with Moslem slaves and mistresses (Isaiah Tishby, *Mishnat Hazohar,* Mosad Bialik, Jerusalem, Vol. 2, 1961, p. 626; hereafter: *M.H.*).

Epstein contends that, while the betrothed concubine found a place in the practice of oriental and Spanish Jews, "the free concubine, not being betrothed . . . found favorable ground everywhere, in Spain as in Germany, in the Orient as in Central Europe" (*Concubine,* p. 186). There is little evidence, however, that the practice among the Ashkenazic Jews was nearly as sexually permissive as among the Sephardim. H. J. Zimmels, in his comparison of their law and practice, writes, "In general . . . their moral and religious conduct when compared with that of the Sephardim in those days was on a much higher level. . . . No case of concubinage is ever mentioned in the *Responsa* of the Ashkenazi Rabbis of those days. Such an institution as the *Berore Averoth* found in Spain, whose task was to guard the moral life of the Jews, was completely strange to German Jewry" (*Ashkenazim and Sephardim,* Oxford University Press, London, 1958, pp. 253-54; hereafter: *Ashkenazim;* see also his discussion of the problems of contact with non-Jewish women which follows there). Falk is in general agreement with this position, though not as categorical (*Matrimonial,* p. 34). Of the 788 *responsa* of Rabbi Meir of Rothenberg (1215?-1293) edited by Irving Agus, only eight deal with problems of sexual laxity, and none of these relates to sexual activities by the unmarried (*Rabbi Meir of Rothenberg,* Dropsie College, Philadelphia, 1947, two volumes). A similar check is provided by the study of the writings of the *Maharil,* Rabbi Jacob Molin (1360-1427). Although there is evidence here, too, of sexual laxity, including one case of a child born out of wedlock, there is nothing of concubinage and the sexual misconduct mentioned in the Spanish sources (Sidney Steinman, *Custom and Survival*, Bloch Publishing Co., New York, 1963, p. 51).

Salo Baron calls attention to the contrast between the Jews and their neighbors: "Most Jewish apologists . . . generally boasted of the superiority of Jewish sexual morality over that of Gentiles. In the northern countries especially that contrast seems to have been quite marked . . . A Jewish apologist observed: 'whether old or young, Jews study the Torah and teach their children from infancy to read books, attend houses of prayer, abstain from profanities, but to speak in a clean language and be careful about taking oaths. They also watch their daughters lest they become licentious and run around with rather than stay away from men; thus there is no apparent promiscuity among them . . . But you profane your speech and swear by the name of God . . . and your daughters are licentious, some living in houses of prostitution . . ." (*History*, Vol. IX, p. 128). Of course, Jewish prostitutes are not unknown, as Baron indicates in *Community*, Vol. II, pp. 313-14. Again, "Enactments to prevent illicit sex relationships among Jews, or between Jews and Gentiles, as well as the record of practices which produced the laws, would likewise fill a substantial volume. Although Jews, for example, Solomon Duran (1400?-1467), sometimes prided themselves on the fact that 'among all nations you will find no nation as free of fornication as is Israel,' the rabbis themselves had to admit that in Spain and northern Africa there were 'a great many lawbreakers entertaining forbidden relationships with Gentile women; even intercourse with an unmarried daughter of Israel has become to them a permissible matter.' One may readily discount some such statements in the sources as due to exaggerations of puritanical preachers and moralists, but they certainly reflect the existence of some all-too-human shortcomings which more recent generations were eager to gloss over. The medieval rabbis preferred to face them, realizing well enough that sex ethics in the ghetto was, in any case, superior to that of its environment" (*Community*, Vol. II, pp. 311-12). Contrast the tone of this statement with his confident assertion that despite Christian-Moslem sexual immoralities in the early period of Islam, the rabbis had effectively stopped such activities in the Jewish community (*History*, Vol. III, p. 143).

Sexual problems were not confined to Spain. We read of a *takkanah* of the community of Candia in 1238 to keep men from the homes of their betrothed because, apparently, pregnancies were not uncommon. Interestingly enough, this enactment resulted from the visit of an

Ashkenazic rabbi, one Baruch ben Isaac, who had passed through Crete on his way to the land of Israel (Finkelstein, *Self-Government,* text on pp. 271-72 and p. 279, comments on pp. 83-84, including the observation that this practice was almost unknown in France and Germany because of the youthful marriages there). Samuel Asaf has gathered much relevant material concerning the practice of other Mediterranean Jewish communities. Isaiah of Trani (early thirteenth-century Italian) mentions the Rumanian custom of cohabitation between the engaged, which he decries. Similar voices are heard in the fifteenth and sixteenth centuries, and the pattern was ended only when the Spanish refugees came into these communities. In Italy and Sicily this also happened. Ovadiah of Bertinoro (1450-1510) writes, when describing his trip to the land of Israel, that in Palermo "most of the betrothed girls come to the bridal canopy pregnant" (pp. 170-71 in Samuel Asaf, "Lehayei Hamishpahah shel Yehudei Bitzantz," *Jubilee Volume for Professor Krauss,* Jerusalem, 1937).

This practice can hardly be compared with the problems of Spanish Jewry. Where the only complaint is that the betrothed couple has not waited for the marriage proper, we are dealing with a far less disturbing situation than that of the mistresses and prostitutes, Jewish and non-Jewish, who existed among Spanish Jewry. There is one more efflorescence of such sexual freedom, although the problem is almost entirely one of prostitution. Cecil Roth writes, "There was no other time, and no other place, in which amorous offenses make their appearance in Jewish life to the extent that they do in fifteenth century Florence, where out of eighty-eight cases tried before the civic magistrates at this time, seventeen were for gambling and thirty-four for moral misdemeanors! There was no other time, and no other place, in which the establishment of a disorderly house in the Jewish quarter could even have been discussed" (*The History of the Jews of Italy,* Jewish Publication Society, Philadelphia, 1946, p. 211). This statement may be somewhat exaggerated, since a defense of Jewish prostitutes had been made in Spain on the ground that intercourse with a non-Jewess involved a danger to life from the non-Jewish authorities. See Zimmels, *Ashkenazim,* pp. 254-55, and the Baron reference on prostitutes above. Roth himself seems to be aware of this fact, as he specifically notes in a fuller treatment of this theme (*The Jews in the Renaissance,* Jewish Publication Society, Philadelphia, 1959, p. 45). Yet even here he summarizes, "Nevertheless, there can be no doubt that in the vast majority of cases the traditional moral standards continued to prevail for ordinary men and women." Salo Baron, in the material on prostitutes noted above, says that the *takkanah* of Forli in 1418, which describes the community as involved in licentious activity and charges the leaders to uproot it, is one indication of the way in which the Renaissance life style influenced the Jewish community. See particularly the Hebrew text, p. 286, and the commentary on pp. 88-89 in Finkelstein, *Self-Government*. Finkelstein also gives an enactment in 1642 of the community of Corfu against betrothed couples meeting, which shows that the laxity of the previous period did not permanently affect Italian Jewry (*ibid.*, pp. 97, 316-17, 319-21).

64. Hayim David Chavel, *Kitvei Rabenu Mosheh ben Nahman*, Mosad Harav Kuk, Jerusalem, Vol. 1, 1963, pp. 381-82; hereafter: *Nahman*.

65. The conflict between the two masters may be traced in another way. Maimonides had made a listing, with comments, of what he took to be the 613 traditional, basic commandments. This was done about 1170, before he wrote his great code. In his *Sefer Hamitzvot* (Shurkin reprint, Brooklyn, 1955) Maimonides lists as negative commandment 355, the prohibition against intercourse without contract and rites, basing himself on the prohibition against the *kedeshah*. He also notes a similar commandment not to give one's daughter to prostitution, which is understood by rabbinic tradition as not giving one's daughter to a man for intercourse except for marital purposes. Maimonides then points out that the reasons given for these two commandments are important because, while the commandments deal with cases of money or exchange and there are commandments dealing with seduction or rape, there is nothing explicit when the two parties have agreed to have intercourse. (This is the earliest mention of mutual consent known to me.) Here, however, the reasons for the commandments, which speak of defiling the earth by such actions, must be understood to include a prohibition against those who are acting by mutual consent (*ibid.*, p. 56).

Nahmanides, in his commentary to this commandment, boldly argues that it does not apply to the man involved, since the language specifically relates to the woman in one case or to the father's act of giving his daughter, in the other. The latter half of that commandment refers to the Jewish court and its responsibilities to curtail immorality, and the commandment thus is related only to those who are expected to keep the woman from doing wrong (see Nahmanides' commentary *ad loc.*). The general argument is carried on at greater length in his

comments to the fifth general principle for deciding what commandments are to be included in the basic 613. Nahmanides insists that
the explanatory phrases which Maimonides takes only as reasons for the
commandments are often separate commandments in themselves. He
cites a number of cases, particularly those empowering the local court
to stop immorality. Yet he now argues that in the case of the phrase
"and do not pollute the land," which concludes the commandment
against prostitutes, we have a warning to the man who might have
intercourse with her (p. 31, para. 10). He further indicates that the
phrase refers equally to a girl who willingly undertakes free intercourse and is not so given by her father, for that case too is not cov-
ered under the commandment proper (*ibid.,* para. 12). All this, he then
insists, has nothing to do with two adult Jews eligible for marriage
with one another, since he interprets harlotry only in terms of disqualification from marrying a priest: "But if they are eligible for marriage and two adults desire a *pilegesh* relationship, it is my intention
to say that they may live together and have intercourse and this is
permitted . . . but not if he has accidental intercourse with her in
the form of prostitution. Such a case comes neither under the commandment of prostitution nor giving one's daughter to prostitution
. . . but under R. Eliezer ben Jacob's rule concerning the eventual
possibility of incest" (p. 62, para. 14). The position taken by each of
the two men is, of course, essentially the same, but now we can understand something of the systematic legal thinking which gave rise to
it and recognize the difficulties anyone faced who wanted to cite a
specific basis for the prohibition of the *pilegesh.*

66. Epstein details the status of the betrothed concubine but does
not do so for the free one. I am not certain that there are two such
distinct types, although it seems clear from the legal literature that
various kinds of relationships did arise involving slaves, converts, and
betrothal. Note that Nahmanides can speak of "marrying" her, even
though he specifically says there are no rites performed. See Epstein,
Concubinage, p. 185.

67. The case of the *pilegesh* in medieval times closely parallels that
of the contemporary love ethic in its most stable form. Anyone seriously
interested in knowing what bearing the Jewish tradition might have
on such relationships today would want to study the relevant data,
particularly the authoritative decisions in specific cases which came
before the judges. Such an investigation takes on special interest because the attitude of the rabbis involved was by no means unanimous,

either in final judgment or in the reasons advanced to validate individual decisions.

In tracing the development of Jewish legal opinion relative to the *pilegesh,* I am turning first to an extensive collection of *responsa* by Solomon ben Adret (1235-1310), one of the great scholars of his time. The cases in his *responsa* which are relevant to our question all involve some kind of betrothal, in most cases with a former servant. We are therefore dealing with the betrothed, not the free, concubine. Thus, Vol. I, ques. 610, discusses the case of a servant who conceived, but no specific mention is made of concubinage. If one holds to the theory that there was an institutionalized pattern called "the betrothed concubine," the relationship here is of this kind, though less in the question than in the response. Similarly, in I, 1205, we have a question about a man who freed his non-Jewish slave, converted her to Judaism, and married her to be his second wife. Again there are rough parallels and no direct statement about concubinage. In II, 363, the questioner speaks of a woman who had been betrothed but received no contract and asks whether her children inherit from their father. Here Solomon specifically calls her a *pilegesh,* but since the case deals only with the rights of her children, he gives us no special data on his attitude toward the relationship with her. His views emerge clearly in IV, 314, which discusses a case concerning a Jewish servant who was seduced by her master after his wife had been barren ten years. He claimed he did this to fulfill the commandment of procreation, and he married the girl after the conception. While the question concerns the legitimacy of the child, Solomon uses the occasion to set forth his attitude toward the *pilegesh.* He follows Maimonides completely, utilizing both verses cited by Maimonides in the *Sefer Hamitzvot* (see above, note 65). He also utilizes Nahmanides' reasoning concerning the girl who gives herself to such a relationship, though Nahmanides made an exception for the *pilegesh* pattern, as we have seen. He says flatly, "Now let me say that I have not come into the legal arena to issue permissions and to make such innovations as to permit marrying [sic] a Jewess as a *pilegesh.* How much the more is that true in a case where he already has a legitimate wife who was properly married to him. For since the Torah was given, the law has evolved, and the *pilegesh* is forbidden. She may be defined as a woman who is set aside particularly for one man but without marital rites or contract. . . ." This statement hardly seems to indicate that Solomon ben Adret thought in terms of a "betrothed" concubine. In any case, he is flatly opposed to the institution, though he admits that it is a postbiblical development in Jewish law. However, see also V, 242 (*She. Utesh. Rashba.*, Benei Berak 1958-Jerusalem 1960, Vols. 1-7).

The *responsa* of Asher ben Yehiel (1250-1327) reflect the Spanish situation. Rubric 32, ques. 13 deals with the issues involved in sexual relations with one's servant and raises the question "whether the family is permitted a legal protest that she stay with him, for it is a blemish on the family that she should be his *pilegesh*." Asher is even firmer in his answer than Solomon ben Adret had been. He says that in such a case, "we do not require the family to make a protest, but the local court should coerce him to send her out of his house, for it is certain that she will be ashamed to go to the ritual bath, and he will then become involved in the heinous sin of intercourse with a woman technically still menstruating." The reasoning is familiar from the conclusion of Nahmanides' *responsum* (see pp. 45-46) and argues for action on the ground of the greater evil which may be caused if the situation is not radically altered. The questioner's comment on the family blemish repeats the argument of the Talmud concerning the refusal to let the unmarried girl stand or even talk with the man who desired her (see above, note 47). This social aspect of the problem is not a matter to be taken lightly, though Asher does not pick it up for the purposes of his legal decision. Hayyim Schauss illustrates and confirms the importance of this social aspect when he says that in the Middle Ages, "the amount of the dowry was less essential [to a match] than the genealogical record and the social position of the family" (*Lifetime*, p. 159). Speaking of a somewhat later period, after the expulsion from Spain in 1492, Jacob Katz writes, "Some weight—although very limited—was placed on a good lineage, i.e., descent from prominent scholars or other famous personages. In contrast, an apostasy or sexual irregularity in the family constituted a stain which had to be compensated for by other considerations" (*Tradition*, p. 138).

Two other *responsa* of Asher relate to this theme. In 37, 1, he objects to the practice of betrothing a concubine and living with her, but his grounds are the same (the fear of menstrual intercourse). Again he urges the community to take action against this practice. The case of 35, 10, involves a subsequent marriage, complete even as to contract. Here Asher is concerned not that the woman was ever the man's concubine but that, having been betrothed by him, she now did not have a divorce from that man before marrying a second man. Both cases seem to be evidence favoring the concept of a "betrothed" concubine (*She. Utesh. Harosh.*, Grossman, New York, 1954).

Jacob ben Asher (1270-1343) adds little to what his father has already said in the first *responsum*, quoted above. He includes the *pilegesh* relationship, though not by name, in a specification of improper sexual styles and flatly says that the court should coerce a man in such a situation until he sends the woman forth, quoting his father's *responsum* verbatim as the basis of his opinion (*Tur Even Haezer*, 26:1).

68. A *responsum* of Nissim ben Reuben Gerondi of Barcelona (1340-1380) is more permissive. A Jewish servant girl was impregnated by her master's son, "after which he gave her a house and furniture and went there freely like a man who goes to the house of his *pilegesh* . . . ." About twenty months after the birth of the child, another man wanted to marry her. The question is whether the normal rule of waiting three months to see if she is pregnant by the previous relationship applies to her. Obviously, as we have seen above and shall see again, it was not uncommon for a woman who had once been a *pilegesh* to marry properly later.

Nissim responds that she must indeed wait the three months, for "she is presumed to be in the status of a *pilegesh* and cannot be termed a wanton woman (*mezanah*). A *pilegesh* who sets herself aside for one man cannot be called wanton, for she is permitted to him. Even the biblical patriarchs had them . . ." (*She. Utesh. Haran.*, Sadilokov, 1944, question 65).

A pupil of Nissim's, Isaac ben Sheshet Barfat (1326-1408), received a similar inquiry on the problem of a *pilegesh* waiting to be married. The inquiry points to the view that "a 'wanton woman does not have to wait the three months to see if she is pregnant, because it is assumed that she watches herself to see that she does not conceive. So a raped or seduced girl does have to wait,' thus far his words. Now in the case of this former *pilegesh* we can be certain that she did not guard against conception but, on the contrary, desired it." Isaac rules that "this *pilegesh* lived with her lover (*hashukah*) as a woman lives with her husband. Hence, she does not herself consider this prostitution, so that she would guard against conception. On the contrary, she wants to conceive so that she may have children who will lend respectability to the relationship. Thus, it is clear that she must wait three months to marry" (*She. Utesh. Bar Sheshet.*, Mefitzei Torah, New York, 1954, item 213).

This *responsum* provides only limited insight into the nature of the relationship. Isaac's opinion on its legitimacy is found in *responsum* 395. The man involved took an oath, contained in a formal document, that he would never take a *pilegesh* or a mistress (*hashukah*) as long as his wife was alive, on penalty of being under the ban of all Jewish communities. (Clauses pledging not to take a *pilegesh* or a second wife were not uncommon among Sephardim, since the ban on polygamy was not in effect among them. See Epstein, *JMC,* p. 272; and Falk, *Matrimonial,* pp. 10 ff.) Later, "lewd urges lured him astray," and he took a certain widow, previously punished by the community for adultery, and set her aside as his mistress (*hashukah*), without marriage contract or rites. In the list of questions which he asks about this case, R. Hisdai ben Solomon of Toledo calls this relationship a sin because the man should not be alone with a woman unless he has properly married her.

In his response, R. Isaac refutes the conceivable arguments for legitimizing the *pilegesh.* As Maimonides had done against Abraham ben David of Posquieres (translated on p. 44), he points out that King David and his court (sic) made the rule against being alone with an adult Jewess after the affair of Tamar and Absalom. This rule made a *pilegesh* relationship impossible. David had taken his concubines before the rule was formulated, and though Solomon took his concubines afterward, he transgressed the law, because he also took many wives. More important, there are no cases of a *pilegesh* relationship after this. R. Isaac agrees with Maimonides that there is a negative commandment in the Torah against it, and he cites Nahmanides, Moses of Coucy, and Isaac of Corbeil as all insisting that the positive commandment to take a wife by rites and contract also applies here. A man must not marry, but "if he wishes to take a woman, he is required to do so by full marital process for every woman he takes. Even if he should take a hundred women, he is required to carry out this positive commandment with each one of them and to make the betrothal blessing. If he had intercourse with any one of them without the marital process, he transgresses that positive commandment. If he sets her aside for himself as a *pilegesh,* how much the more is it a transgression of this commandment, for a woman who lives with a man without being married to him may be whipped at the order of the court," i.e., she too is transgressing a command.

The prohibition is sweeping and complete. He has tried to leave no room for any kind of rebuttal or exception. He is "very strict in his halachic decisions" (*The Jewish Encyclopedia,* article "Isaac ben Sheshet," Vol. 6, p. 632).

Another fourteenth-century authority to deal with this question receives the opposite description. Louis Ginzberg, in discussing Menahem ben Aaron ben Zerah (d. 1385), says that his work "occupies a peculiar position among codes, and is in a certain sense unique. As the author states in the introduction . . . it is intended mainly for rich Jews who associate with princes and who, on account of their high station and their intercourse with the non-Jewish world, are not overrigorous in regard to Jewish regulations" (*The Jewish Encyclopedia,* article "Menahem b. Aaron ben Zerah," Vol. 8, p. 466). The book involved is *Tzeidah Laderekh,* and the material on the *pilegesh* is found in Rubric 1, Essay 3, Chap. 2 (p. 136 in the Warsaw 1880 edition).

Menahem cites the Maimonides text but uses the gloss of Abraham ben David of Posquieres to permit the *pilegesh.* He then cites the *responsum* of Nahmanides affirming this position but ends his citation of the text before the concluding sentence, in which Nahmanides had urged Rabbi Jonah to use his communal authority to prohibit this practice. He continues, "And because there are many who take a *pilegesh* in this country and betroth them, I have written this to show them their error. Many of them say that they betroth them so that they, the husbands, will not be unfaithful to them. That is a false response, for after saying they do so to stay in purity, they then go and stay away from their city and their homes for a long time, and 'the inclinations of man's heart are evil from his youth.' " He urges them either to take one good wife and live faithfully with her or, if a man must have a mistress, to marry her fully. Since that is often impossible because polygamy is forbidden or because he might have to give his wife a divorce and the attendant divorce settlement, it is really better to have one good wife and stay with her. Yet that pious conclusion sounds somewhat hollow after his earlier statement that "to set aside a woman for himself without any marital rites is permitted."

The last *responsum* available to us from the period before the *Shulhan Arukh* is that of Meir Katzenellenbogen of Padua. He was an Ashkenazi, even though he served in an Italian city. For this reason, his *responsum* is cited as evidence of Ashkenazic as well as Sephardic concubinage (see above, note 63). The question refers to a man who had a *pilegesh* and married her off to another man, who later divorced her. The first man now wishes to take her back, apparently as his concubine, because his first wife is barren and is amenable to this arrangement. He expects her to live "in full purity, so that she will go to the ritual bath and be religiously acceptable. . . ." The questioner, who obviously knows something of the previous legal rulings, wants to know if this arrangement is acceptable. The response deals only with the question of whether there applies here the law forbidding a couple once married to remarry after an intervening divorce and marriage. Yet at the very end Meir says, "It is more seemly [*yoter nakhon*] for him to take this woman by the marriage rites and contract according to the religiously proper usages than that he should take her as his *pilegesh*. Let him rather eat meat of a dying animal which has been ritually slaughtered than that which is found dead in the field, thus he will live to see sons and extend his days." The last sentence is a poetic legal flourish which brings considerable force to bear on the comment. The one kind of meat is *kosher,* the other is specifically forbidden by the Torah. Does the author mean that the *pilegesh* is forbidden in that sense? I think not, otherwise he would not have started out as weakly, as he does, by saying, "It is more seemly. . . ." Yet, since this phrase weakens his statement, he wants to protest against anyone utilizing what he knows he cannot forbid, and so he ends with a strong warning. It is consistent with this interpretation that he never protests the original *pilegesh* relationship (*She. Utesh. Mahari Mintz Umaharam Padva.*, Krakau-Fischer and Deutscher, 1882, p. 64. See the comments on his usual liberality in Max Seligsohn's article "Katzenellenbogen, Meir," *The Jewish Encyclopedia,* Vol. 7, p. 454).

We may then summarize the development of Jewish law in this area over the period from Maimonides to the *Shulhan Arukh* as follows: Maimonides came out strongly against the relationship and was followed in that opinion by Solomon ben Adret, Asher ben Yehiel, Jacob, his son, and Isaac ben Sheshet Barfat. He was opposed by Abraham ben David of Posquieres, Nissim ben Reuben Gerondi, and Menahem ben Aharon Zarhi. Nahmanides opposed Maimonides on legal grounds and argued that the relationship was legally permissible but urged that the community officials use their discretionary powers to suppress it. Meir Katzenellenbogen of Padua similarly considered it legal but immoral. It can be reasonably said, then, that the ruling of the *Shulhan Arukh* may have stated the case in more unconditional language than this background warranted, but it clearly could not have come as a surprise to anyone nor did it seem to be a great departure from the attitudes that were developing before it. And its historical situation, after the catastrophic expulsion of the Jews of Spain, makes that judgment even easier to understand.

69. *Even Haezer,* 26, Introduction and para. 1.

70. The *responsum* of Jacob Emden is an extraordinary document, not only because it is unparalleled in the period following the *Shulhan Arukh* and is written by an Ashkenazic authority. H. J. Zimmels points out the strange turn of events that makes a Sephardic rabbi of the sixteenth century, David ben Zerah, strictly forbid the *pilegesh,* while Emden, whom he calls "the foremost representative of the Ashkenazim," uses the old Sephardic argument, the laxity of contemporaries, to permit it (*Ashkenazim,* p. 258).

What astonishes the reader as much as the decision is the almost unbelievable subjectivity of the author, who consistently refuses to acknowledge the negative stand taken by the various authorities or cannot see in their arguments any of the real strength they possess. Emden is obviously deeply troubled by the sexual immoralities of his time, though with typical rabbinic circumlocution he only hints at them. His ingenious argument, after the legal hurdles are cleared, is that the reinstatement of this provision will serve as "a fence around the law." Normally such a fence would call for more restriction than the thing to be protected. But it is not marriage that Emden is trying to protect, rather it is the moral purity of the people. The *pilegesh* relationship is indeed stricter than the kind of sexual immorality they have been allowing themselves. Yet if it were permitted, they would have legitimate access to a more liberal sexual life, and he indicates conditions under which that would be the case, e.g., when the regular wife is menstruating. One might say that Emden was the Jewish proponent of "new morality" in his time.

Yet it is difficult to believe that he himself did not know that he was radically altering the pattern of Jewish sexual practice. His very last line in the letter is that this is all related to the verse, "it is time to work for the Lord." In the rabbinic interpretation this is the basis in an emergency for changing a law of the Torah. It reads in full: "When it is time to work for the Lord, they may change Thy Torah." It is cited by the rabbis as the justification of writing down the oral law (Tem. 14b). See Jacob Emden, *Sheelat Yavetz,* Gross, New York, 1944, Part 2, ques. 15.

71. One may gain some idea of the general attitude in the community

from several sources. As to the legal attitudes, it is clear that Emden's proposal met with no response. Nor can one find another ruling like his. Samuel ben Uri of Furth (*fl.* 1640-1690) comments that the prohibition of the *pilegesh* is not satisfactorily established and hence the right to punish her as violating a biblical command is not reasonable (*Beit Shemuel, Even Haezer,* 26:1). I assume he is arguing about the theoretical problem of legal construction, under which, in specific categories of rabbinic thought, she legitimately falls. What he says still would not prevent the local court from using, as a basis for punishing her, its general authority to stop immorality. Such theoretical issues seem to be the concern of the other commentators to the *Mishneh Torah,* the *Tur,* and the *Shulhan Arukh* on this matter. A good many of them from the seventeenth to the nineteenth centuries simply skip the *pilegesh* phrases, while those who do treat them are interested in reconciling the divergent definitions of the term (cf. the Yerushalmi and Rashi readings referred to above, note 59) or are seeking to discover why Nahmanides read Maimonides the way he quotes him in his *responsum.*

The *responsa* of this period are largely silent on this topic. Freiman has found only two which are relevant in the entire period from the *Shulhan Arukh* to modern times, and both are negative (*Sefer,* pp. 360-61). We must remember that we are dealing with Ashkenazic communities and sources, and there had never been a tradition of the *pilegesh* among the Ashkenazim.

Actual practice among the Ashkenazic communities in the shtetl/ghetto period is described by Katz, perhaps with too much reliance on the general laws of the *Shulhan Arukh* as against specific community documents: "All sexual contacts and erotic satisfactions outside of monogamous marriage were prohibited" to men as to women. This view, based on the Talmud, became the people's standard through the Jewish ethical writings, which were saturated with the teachings of the Zohar and Kabbala (*Tradition,* p. 138). "Deviations [from the sexual code] occurred not as part of any conscious free thinking, but as temporary lapses regretted by those who committed them. This fact explains the inquiries regarding ways of doing penance for sexual sins, ranging from masturbation to adultery, in which the responsa literature abounds. . . . The fact that the guilty parties themselves asked for severe penances to atone for their sin—and there are cases where the rabbi gave a more severe ruling only in order to pacify the questioner—indicates that although sexual purity did not reign supreme, the ideal itself was firmly entrenched, and that it operated both as a restraining and a corrective force which, even after the deviation, restored the equilibrium" (*ibid.,* pp. 147-48).

These general attitudes maintained themselves in the shtetl through the nineteenth century and into the twentieth. Sex was considered good but in its proper place, which was marriage. The separation of the sexes was maintained as a barrier against immorality, though some were somewhat nonchalant about it and others rather fanatic. Teen-age marriages were still the norm (*Life Is With People,* Zborowski and Herzog, Schocken Books, New York, 1962, pp. 135-37. Cf. Schauss, *Lifetime,* pp. 179-81). That was the experience of most of the Eastern European migrants to the United States in the early part of this century.

72. A special factor making for a stricter view of sexual relationships from the thirteenth century on is the growth of Jewish mysticism. Since something has been said above of the Aristotelian disdain for the body which rendered Jewish philosophy, on the whole, antithetical to sexual activity in general (a view also seen in the ethical literature which derived from it), a word should be said here concerning the attitudes developed in medieval Jewish mysticism. With the expulsion from Spain in 1492 mysticism took hold of many people, especially when compared with the numbers interested in philosophy in the preceding few centuries. After the Hasidic movement of the early eighteenth century it became a direct mass movement. Katz can say of the period from 1500 to 1750, "The height of erotic-cum-religious experience was reached in married life where the influence of the cabala had taught the couple to regard their union as symbolic of parallel processes in the Divine sphere, a concept which became widespread in the period through the cabalist *musar* [ethical] literature, especially the *Sh'lah* [*Two Tables of the Covenant*], of Rabbi Isaiah Horowitz and cognate works" (*Tradition,* p. 145).

Scholem, our major source for the history of Jewish mysticism, notes some aspects of love symbolism in German Hasidism from about 1150 to 1250 (Gershom G. Scholem, *Major Trends in Jewish Mysticism,* Schocken Books, New York, 1946, p. 96) but finds the explicit appearance of sexual symbolism in the doctrine of the Zohar, about 1275 (*ibid.,* pp. 225 ff.). What is essentially involved in sex, as in all other human actions, is the direct effect of human behavior on the inner workings of the Divine in its dynamic manifestation as the *Ten Sefirot.* Since these involve a masculine and a feminine principle (in God himself, so to speak), properly intended human sexual intercourse helps the Divine *Sefirot* to achieve that fullness of harmony and integration among themselves which is characterized by the unity of the male and female principles. Thus, when man's intercourse is holy, God is, as it were, unified; but when man's sexual activity is immoral, God's inner dynamic is disrupted. No wonder Jewish mysticism had such a strong effect upon strengthening traditional Jewish sexual standards. (For an English account of the Zoharic theory, see A. E. Waite, *The Holy Kabbalah,* University Books, New Hyde Park, N.Y., 1960, pp. 377-402.)

Tishby puts the moral effect this way: "Seeing the situation of the human male and female as the mirror image of the structure of the Divine energies confers a distinctly sacred character to married life, especially the sexual act itself, which in this world depicts and concretizes the Divine intercourse and even aids its accomplishment, drawing benefit from it to the creatures here below" (*M. H.,* Vol. 2, p. 609). His summary is particularly useful because of the many citations which he gives from the Zohar itself. In this particular connection see the sections "kidush hazivug," p. 640, and "zivug hatzadik im hashekhinah," p. 643. The content of the teaching is quite specific, and it is important for an age emerging from collective prudery such as ours to understand how seriously the mystics and, following them, much of the Jewish community in these latter centuries took the sanctification of intercourse. Thus the time (preferably midnight; Sabbath, for the pious), place, and manner of intercourse are all set by Divine counterpart (pp. 609, 612). "The emission itself should take place in love and never in anger, for to do so in love makes the semen a treasured thing but to do so in anger is to render the intercourse immoral, the equivalent of making a whore of the Divine Presence" (pp. 612, 613). Illicit intercourse causes grave damage to the Divine *Sefirot* (pp. 613-17), but proper intercourse for procreation causes the Divine energies to flow back toward man (p. 613). For the person who prepares to have intercourse, the Zohar recommends a prayer which ends, "I take my stand in the realm of holiness; I garb myself in the holiness of the Divine King" (p. 618).

While several other major sources may be cited (see Epstein, *SLC,* p. 23, and Jacob Katz, "Nisuin Vehayei Ishut Bemotzaei Yemei Habeinayim," *Tziyon,* Tenth Year, pp. 42 ff.), special note should be made of a small pamphlet which was in reasonably wide circulation and dealt solely with the topic of intercourse. Entitled *Igeret Hakodesh ("Letter on Holiness"),* it is attributed to Nahmanides, though, according to

the recent editor of his writings, it was probably written by R. Azriel
ben Menahem (1160-1238). *Nahman,* Vol. 2, p. 318.

The kabbalistic doctrine of human activity influencing the Divine
plays no part in this work. It is almost entirely taken up with a psycho-
somatic theory of procreation. One who wants to have worthy children
should incline his soul and that of his wife toward God during intercourse. Any immoral thoughts or acts on their part will result in unworthy children.

The general attitude of the author is well summed up at the beginning of Chap. 2:

> "intercourse is a holy and pure thing when it is done in an ap-
> propriate way, in an appropriate time, and with an appropriate
> intention. Let no man think that in proper intercourse there is
> anything blameworthy or perverse, Heaven forfend, for inter-
> course is called 'knowing' . . . and if it were not a matter of great
> holiness it would not have been called that. The matter is cer-
> tainly not as Maimonides thought, as described in the *Guide of
> the Perplexed,* where he praises Aristotle for saying that the sense
> of touch is a shame to men. Heaven defend us from such errors.
> The matter is certainly not as the Greek has said, for there is in
> this discussion a touch of heresy. . . . But we, the children of the
> masters of the holy Torah, believe that God created all things
> according to the wisdom of His will . . . and if our sexual organs
> are a disgrace, how could it happen that God created a thing
> which was blemished, shameful, or faulty? . . ."

And the proof is that, when Adam and his wife were naked with one
another before they sinned, they were not embarrassed or ashamed
(p. 323 in the Chavel edition).

The attitude of the Jewish community in late medieval times to
sexual intercourse is well summarized in the prayer it prescribed before
beginning the act. The following translation is taken from a collection
of prayers, *Sefer Likutei Tzevi,* published in Sulzbach in 1797 (p. 126).
It ascribes the prayer to Nahmanides, but it is likely to have been of
later origin: "O Lord my God and God of my fathers, ground of all
the universes, for the sake of Your great and holy name alluded to in
the verse, 'The Lord has remembered us; He will bless, He will bless
the house of Israel, He will bless the house of Aaron,' may it be Your
will that You emanate from Your spirit of power unto me and give me

might and strength in my organs and my body that I might regularly fulfill the commandment pertaining to my sexual cycle [*onati*]; that there be not found in my organs, body, or passion any weakness or slackness; that there be no forcing, unseemly thought, confusion of mind, or weakening of power to prevent me from fulfilling my desire with my wife. Rather, now and forever, let my passion be ready for me without fail or slackness of organ, at any time that I should desire. Amen Selah." A much longer paragraph then follows which is a prayer for a healthy, faithful male offspring. The prayer is supposed to be recited three times, adjacent to one's bed, "in holiness, purity, and cleanliness." (I am indebted to Rabbi A. Stanley Dreyfus for locating the text of this prayer.)

73. A good example is the explanation given for not having a *pilegesh* relationship. Let us summarize some of the most important reasons. Maimonides says it is against the biblical law prohibiting prostitution. For Nahmanides it is, in effect, morally repugnant, for it will cause immorality in the community. (Recall that he said the general prohibition of unmarried intercourse does not apply here because the parentage is clear.) Asher says it will lead to menstrual intercourse. Isaac ben Sheshet Barfat says it contravenes the laws of being alone with an adult woman. Obviously, almost all of these are legal rather than substantive reasons; that is, they are designed to fit an individual case into a legal system of rules and precedents rather than to deal with the values implicit in the act of intercourse and see how it relates to a general view of man and society. If we dealt only with the reasons given by authorities, we could, if precedent did not swamp logic, overcome all but Nahmanides with ease. Our Jewish guidance is less the reasons given by the judges than it is what they did and its own general context of faith and value.

Legal reasoning is, of course, not without its philosophical overtones. Indeed, there is a general sense of value implicit in the laws, and this, as well as the specific rules and cases, determines what the judge will do. In a religious law such as Judaism the two are closely interrelated. The philosophic side of the legal data given in this chapter is brought out in my personal statement at the end of the book. For the general problem, see Isaac Heinemann, *Taamei Hamitzvot,* Vol. 1, p. 34.

74. Peah 17a.

75. Freiman (*Sefer,* p. 396) records Rabbi Jacob Toledano's proposal of 1930 to revive the *pilegesh* in order to obviate certain difficulties which under the rabbinic laws of divorce arise after a fully proper

marriage. To keep moral standards high and take care of social responsibility (e.g., inheritance), he suggested it be done only under the supervision of the local Jewish court. The proposal was speedily criticized and withdrawn. The language of the critic is of some interest. He insists that "it is forbidden to proclaim such a thing and even more so to publish it abroad."

Zeev W. Falk similarly suggested that the problems involved in the marriage of a member of a priestly family to a divorced woman might be resolved by permitting them to establish an officially sanctioned *pilegesh* relationship. Again, the response was tumultuous and negative. Moreover, it was not only the substance of the legal argument which was attacked but the very mention of such a possibility before a public unaware that Jewish law had ever allowed for such relationships. The original essay and the later response to the critics have been collected in the little volume *Halakhah Umaaseh Bemedinat Yisrael*, Wahrmann, Jerusalem, 1967. The relevant passages are on pp. 60 ff.

The response of the critics to the Toledano and Falk proposals seems more characteristic of traditional Jewish attitudes toward sexual matters than most modern writers seem prepared to admit. The frequent discussions of Jewish healthy-mindedness in this area give one the impression that a good deal of the modern candor and openness toward sex already existed in the Jewish sources. The truth would rather seem to be that the Freudian revolution has been widely accepted in the Jewish community, and modern Jewish writers, drawn by the need for apologetics, have broadly overstated the true nature of traditional Jewish acceptance of man's sexual nature and needs.

Two recent publications seem to be fairly representative of the customary Jewish approach to such matters. In his treatment of the source materials in *Sex and the Family in the Jewish Tradition* (Burning Bush Press, New York, 1967), Robert Gordis does not mention the *pilegesh* relationship at all and draws a general conclusion about premarital intercourse in Jewish law, with one exception, from data concerned with the sexual relations of betrothed couples (*ibid.*, pp. 41, 56-57). Another writer, Rabbi Pinchas Stolper, limits himself to the statement that "everything related to the urges, emotions and organs associated with the act of creating a child must be kept strictly within the walls of the home and married life. By everything, we necessarily mean *every and any* act of physical contact between the sexes, as well as the guarding of the privacy and hiddenness of the body of the woman, in accordance with the *tsnius* (modesty) standards set by Jewish law" (*The Road to Responsible Jewish Adulthood,* Union of Orthodox Jewish Congregations of America, Youth Division, New York, 1967, p. 27).

76. See the discussion and literature on this general theme in Hettlinger, *Living,* pp. 156-57, notes 16-19, and p. 168, note 15. His defense of Kinsey in this area seems reasonable but should be taken within the context of the criticism.

77. While their material is limited to those facts discovered in empirical studies and therefore hardly likely to deal with so unobservable a matter as "the whole person," see the findings relative to the difference between humans and animals as regards sexual activity, particularly items A 2 and A 3.1 in Berelson and Steiner, *Human Behavior,* Harcourt, Brace and World, 1964, p. 300 (hereafter: *Behavior*).

78. This is not a theoretical suggestion but the advice given by Dr. Albert Ellis, one of the protagonists of a freer sexual life. In an interview he suggested "that romance was not lasting and that to keep a marriage together adultery might be a good thing for some couples" (*New York Times,* Sept. 7, 1967, p. 27). In Denmark people who approve of premarital intercourse also tended to approve extramarital intercourse (Harold T. Christensen, "Scandinavian and American Sex Norms," in Reiss, *Journal,* pp. 62 and 64 and the note on the latter. Bell interprets a similar positive correlation found by Kinsey among Americans in *Premarital,* p. 150).

79. Almost all societies recognize this and seek to enforce it in some sort of way. For the Jewish point of view, somewhat apologetically presented, see K. Kahana, *The Concept of Marriage in Jewish Law,* E. J. Brill, Leiden, 1966. He says, "Marriage cannot be the concern only of the partners to it. The community as a whole is directly involved in every marriage because the interests of every person are affected by that marriage" (p. 37). In this way the wife is now prohibited to all other men, the incest lines are drawn, the legitimacy of children is established, and the possibility of inheritance, fixed. That is why witnesses should be understood as appearing to represent the rights of the community at a wedding.

80. Jacob Emden in the *responsum* referred to above actually uses this phrase or its equivalent several times.

81. Note that it is a demonstrable scientific fact that "Premarital sexual relations are allowed in a clear majority of human societies. . . ."

But in view of the preceding discussion also note the conclusion of that statement, "but extramarital relations are almost universally condemned" (Berelson and Steiner, *Behavior,* p. 300).

82. Here are the words of Philo on this topic, written about 1900 years ago (the English version may seem somewhat rhetorical in flavor, but rhetoric was apparently the style of the day): "The corruption of a maiden is a criminal offense . . . which some whose way it is to bedizen ugly things with specious terms, ashamed to admit its true nature, give the name of love. Still the kinship does not amount to complete similarity, because the wrong caused by the corruption is not passed on to several families as it is with adultery, but is concentrated in one, that of the maiden herself. Our advice then to one who desires a damsel of gentle birth should be this: 'My good sir, have nothing to do with reckless and shameless effrontery or treacherous snares, or anything of the kind, and do not either openly or secretly prove yourself a rascal. But if you have heart and soul, center your affections on the girl, go to her parents, if they are alive, or, if not, to her brothers or guardians or others who have charge of her, lay bare before them the state of your affections, as a free man should, ask her hand in marriage and plead that you may not be thought unworthy of her. For none of those who have had the care of the girl would behave so stupidly as to set himself in opposition to the increasing earnestness of your entreaties, particularly if, on examination, he finds that your affections are not counterfeited nor superficial, but are genuine and firmly established" (*The Special Laws,* III, 65-68).

83. Much of this material has been annotated above (see note 63). Nothing has been said thus far about the possibility of letting the act of intercourse itself serve as the equivalent of betrothal, which apparently was once Jewish practice and is still a part of rabbinic law. The first statement in the Mishnah tractate on betrothal lists intercourse as one of the three ways of acquiring a wife. The rabbinic tradition on this matter, on which there are extensive data, is summed up by the classic commentator to the Mishnah, Ovadiah of Bertinoro (1450-1510): "Even though one does not find in the Torah specific acts for acquiring a wife more clear than that of intercourse, the sages have said that one who contracts intercourse in this way should be punished at the order of the court so that Jews should not become morally dissolute." (For the background, see Boaz Cohen, *Roman,* p. 287 and note 33; and Falk, *Matrimonial,* p. 38.) The attitude of the rabbis toward those who engaged in this practice seems quite consistent. (For the problem with the

Judeans in early rabbinic times, see Epstein, *JMC,* p. 73; *SLC,* pp. 126-31; and Falk, *Matrimonial,* pp. 44 ff.)

84. Though the song about the "Woman of Valor" (Prov. 31:10-31) cannot be taken as more significant than the vast biblical data on fecundity, it is noteworthy that it praises her for many things but does not find it necessary to mention among them the number of children she produced.

85. Song of Sol. 8:6.

86. The new morality, or situation ethics, has so far not been discussed in this book because, after all the polemics against rules and legalism are exhausted, ethical analysis must still clarify standards of judgment, types of situations, and what they are likely to mean in terms of given standards. I believe James Gustafson is right in seeing this as a somewhat artificial issue. See my summary of the relevant literature in "The New Morality," *Judaism,* Vol. 15, No. 3, Summer 1966. For an example of the way in which the situationist begins to do more generalized ethical reasoning, see Joseph Fletcher, *Moral Responsibility,* Westminster, Philadelphia, 1967, pp. 137-40, a section of the chapter "Ethics and Unmarried Sex" and titled, interestingly enough, "The Solution."

John A. T. Robinson seems far more level-headed. He is somewhat surprised that anyone should feel he is advocating freer sexuality. He is concerned to point out how high a standard love is and how much it would demand of people involved in it. Yet his insistence that love is "the criterion for every form of behavior, inside marriage or out of it. . . . For *nothing else* makes a thing right or wrong," makes it clear that he gives religious sanction to situations of intercourse which have never before been given by the Anglican church (*Honest to God,* Westminster, Philadelphia, 1963, p. 119). Perhaps he is right in asserting that this is what Jesus intended, but he should not be so ingenuous as to wonder why people are shocked or disturbed by his teaching. He is authorizing acts which no Christian authorized before. He has also written that "the nexus between bed and board, between sex and the sharing of life at every level must be pressed as strongly as ever by those who really care for persons as persons . . ." (*Christian Morals Today,* Westminster, Philadelphia, 1964, p. 32). He also talks of the unmarried not having a complete sharing but never indicates why love should lead on to that (*ibid.,* p. 42). There is a hint here that love is more than momentary, and that the fullest love requires the most complete sharing. To me, this hint leads on to form and structure, a theme I have developed in this book. I wonder how Fletcher or Robinson can religiously rather than pragmatically justify marriage if they do not pass beyond their polemics against law.

87. The marriage relationship is one of the two major biblical symbols describing God's relationship to the people of Israel. (The other, more common, one is the straightforward contract symbol, the Covenant.) It is to be found in such places as Ezek. 16:8, Mal. 2:14, and Prov. 2:17. It seems to be the basis of most of the Book of Hosea. Yohanan Muffs has argued in a public lecture that one should see it in the formula "You shall be My people and I will be your God," which is almost certainly a conscious parody of the technical legal formula for acquiring a wife in the ancient Near East. See Falk, *Matrimonial,* pp. 4 and 42; and Schauss, *Lifetime,* p. 130. The opposite also remains true, that sexual immorality is quickly linked with apostasy. This is the burden of Num. 25, and it is a continual rabbinic theme, e.g., San. 63b and 106a.

AFTERWORD

In writing this book I have been troubled by two special problems. The first is style. Most religious writing on practical questions is so "square" that I do not recognize my kind of faith in it. On the other hand, I find most of the popularly accepted religious radicals quite inauthentic. To be true to what I believe has meant studious avoidance of the customary religious rhetoric without surrendering loyalty to that inner vision which founds faith. I sought hardheadedness without sensationalism or cynicism, and to strike this tone seemed to me as critical as the actual substance of the work. I have labored hard at this problem and remain troubled by it. For their help to me in this regard I am grateful to a number of the rabbis who direct Hillel Foundations at various universities and who read a late version of this book. My thanks go to Richard Israel, of Yale University, for devoting time to this task; to Louis Milgrom, of the University of Minnesota, particularly for questioning some of my interpretations of Jewish sources; to Robert Jacobs, of Washington University, whose reflections on the problem of peer groups and values were instructive; and to Max Ticktin, of the University of Chicago, whose sensitive critique of the whole caused me to rework much of it. Their reactions enabled me to see the student's perspective better, and I am grateful that their years of experience were made available to me. Drs. Nahum Glatzer, of Brandeis University, and Philip Rieff, of the University of Pennsylvania, who also read the manuscript, commented on it primarily from the standpoint of its intellectual adequacy and made a number of valuable suggestions. None of these gracious critics bears any responsibility for what I finally determined to do and to risk.

I was, at the same time, concerned with another problem. I have argued that Jewish tradition should be our primary but not our absolute guide in making commitments in belief and action. Yet how reliable a thesis is that? Is it an assertion of ideology, a rationalization of institutional self-interest, or of truth, even in the necessarily subjective way such truths of value are established today? The only way to answer such a question would be to apply it to a practical issue and see. I think most previous efforts in this direction are unconvincing, for they tend to marshall only that portion of the Jewish evidence which points in the direction the researcher wishes to go. Judaism is too dynamic and dialectical for such treatment. If the tradition is relevant, it must be so in its diversity and development. Consequently, I have undertaken this study as a test of that thesis. All the ingredients of modernity are present: a skeptical audience, a problem alive with overtones of freedom and emancipation, and an open-minded approach to the Jewish source materials.

I do not know how others will react either to my substantive suggestions about sexual conduct or to my handling of the inter-relations of modern culture, general ethics, Jewish tradition and faith. For myself I know that this work represents a positive culmination to my writings of recent years in search of a new path in Jewish theology. That a question of action should be the means of testing the adequacy of my understanding of my Jewish belief seems to me quite appropriate.

Several people deserve more thanks than I can here suitably express. Dr. Julius Kravetz, the most generous of colleagues, was kind enough to start me through the thicket of *halachic* materials in this area and then read the chapter "The Jewish Experience," saving me from several errors. Dr. Alfred Jospe, Director of Program and Resources for the B'nai B'rith Hillel Foundations, insisted that I write this book and refused to allow any of the numerous problems which arose to keep it from completion. He then brought to the delicate task of producing a manuscript that would be as useful to its audience as it was authentic to its author, energy, determination, sensitivity, and high standards. I am indebted to Mr. John Thornton of Schocken Books, who edited the book for style. Jean Paxton brought intelligence and care to the continual retyping of the manuscript. The library staff of the Hebrew Union College-Jewish Institute of Religion in New York was kind enough to pull out many a book from distant and even dangerous places in our overcrowded stacks, while others made photocopies of numerous critical pages for me to study and restudy at my convenience. Most of the best things in this book I have learned from living in the climate of honesty and good humor created by my wife and three daughters. Yet all that was made possible by Him whom our forebears knew not only as Father and as King but as Teacher.

Barukh atah Adonai hamelamed torah leamo yisrael.

"I call you blessed, Adonai, for teaching Torah to your people Israel."

EUGENE B. BOROWITZ

Hebrew Union College–
Jewish Institute of Religion
The New York School

SUGGESTIONS FOR FURTHER READING

Bell, Robert R. *Premarital Sex in a Changing Society.* A comprehensive, clearly presented summary and interpretation of the research data gathered in this century on premarital sexual practices. For openness to fact and avoidance of sensationalism, this book serves as a model for study and evaluation.

Brown, Norman O. *Life Against Death.* A useful, because wide-ranging, introduction to Freud's theory of human sexuality (see especially Part Two). Other works of similar scope and perceptiveness are Ernest Jones's 3-volume *Life and Work of Sigmund Freud* (New York: Basic Books, 1953-1957; also available in a 1-volume abridged paperback edition) or Philip Rieff's *Freud, the Mind of the Moralist* (Garden City, N.Y.: Doubleday & Co., 1961).

Diamond, Malcolm. *Martin Buber: Jewish Existentialist* (London: Oxford University Press, 1960). I have cited none of Buber's works either in the notes or the bibliography, yet his sense of what it is to be a person suffuses much of what has been said here. Diamond offers the most direct access to his thought.

Epstein, Louis. *Sex Laws and Customs in Judaism.* The classic modern treatment of Jewish attitudes and practices in this area. Somewhat dated by the author's insistence on imaginative reconstructions of the past and apologetics for the tradition he loves. Nonetheless interesting and indispensable.

Group for the Advancement of Psychiatry. *Sex and the College Student.* Another model of sensitive intelligence and rich experience applied to an exceedingly complex problem so as to produce genuine wisdom. Provides a mature understanding of the emotional aspects of sexual activity.

Hettlinger, Richard. *Living With Sex: The Student's Dilemma.* Of all the books in the contemporary literature of sexual guidance this one seems most appealing. The author knows the college student well, faces his problems realistically, speaks to him out of an honest equality, and never loses his high sense of what a human being ought to be.

BIBLIOGRAPHY

THERE IS an almost unlimited amount of material relative to sex, ethics, and sex ethics. This bibliography is limited to the publications cited in this volume.

BOOKS

Abrahams, Israel. *Jewish Life in the Middle Ages*. Philadelphia: Jewish Publication Society, 1896.

Agus, Irving. *Rabbi Meir of Rothenberg*. 2 vols. Philadelphia: Dropsie College, 1947.

Ardrey, Robert. *The Territorial Imperative*. New York: Atheneum, 1966.

Baer, Yitzhak. *A History of the Jews in Christian Spain*. Vols. I-II. Philadelphia: Jewish Publication Society, 1966.

Baron, Salo. *The Jewish Community*. Vols. I-III. Philadelphia: Jewish Publication Society, 1942.

Baron, Salo. *A Social and Religious History of the Jews*. Vols. I-IX. Philadelphia: Jewish Publication Society, 1952-1965.

Belkin, Samuel. *Philo and the Oral Law*. Cambridge, Mass.: Harvard University Press, 1940.

Bell, Robert R. *Premarital Sex in a Changing Society*. Englewood Cliffs, N.J.: Prentice-Hall, 1966.

Berelson and Steiner. *Human Behavior*. New York: Harcourt, Brace and World, Inc., 1964.

Blackman, Philip. *Mishnayoth*. New York: The Judaica Press, Inc., 1965.

Borowitz, Eugene B. *A New Jewish Theology in the Making*. Philadelphia: Westminster Press, 1968.

Borowitz, Eugene B. *What Can a Jew Say About Faith Today?* Philadelphia: Westminster Press, 1969.

Brown, Driver, and Briggs. *Hebrew and English Lexicon of the Old Testament*. London: Oxford University Press, 1906.

177

Brown, Norman O. *Life Against Death.* Middletown, Conn.: Wesleyan University Press, 1959.

Cohen, Boaz. *Jewish and Roman Law.* New York: Jewish Theological Seminary of America, 1966.

Danby, Herbert. *The Mishnah.* London: Oxford University Press, 1933.

de Vaux, Roland. *Ancient Israel.* New York: McGraw-Hill, 1961.

Duvall, Evelyn Millis. *Why Wait Till Marriage?* New York: Association Press, 1965.

Ehrmann, Winston. *Premarital Dating Behavior.* New York: Henry Holt and Company, 1959.

Ellis, Albert. *Sex and the Single Man.* New York: Lyle Stuart, 1963.

Ellis, Albert. *Sex Without Guilt.* New York: Lyle Stuart, 1958.

Epstein, Isidore, ed. *The Babylonian Talmud.* London: The Soncino Press, 1936.

Epstein, Louis. *The Jewish Marriage Contract.* New York: Jewish Theological Seminary of America, 1927.

Epstein, Louis. *Sex Laws and Customs in Judaism.* New York: Bloch Publishing Co., 1948.

Falk, Z. W. *Jewish Matrimonial Law in the Middle Ages.* London: Oxford University Press, 1966.

Feldman, David. *Birth Control in Jewish Law.* New York University Press, 1968.

Finkelstein, Louis. *Jewish Self-Government in the Middle Ages.* New York: Philipp Feldheim, Inc., 1964.

Fletcher, Joseph, *Moral Responsibility.* Philadelphia: Westminster Press, 1967.

Freud, Sigmund. *Civilization and Its Discontents.* New York: W. W. Norton & Co., 1962.

Fromm, Erich. *The Heart of Man.* New York: Harper and Row, 1964.

Ginzberg, Louis. *The Legends of the Jews.* Vols. I-VII. Philadelphia: Jewish Publication Society, 1914-1946.

Goodman, Paul. *Growing Up Absurd.* New York: Random House, 1960.

Gordis, Robert. *Sex and the Family in the Jewish Tradition.* New York: Burning Bush Press, 1967.

Greene, Gael. *Sex and the College Girl.* New York: Dell Publishing Co., 1964.

Group for the Advancement of Psychiatry. *Sex and the College Student.* Report No. 60. New York: GAP, 1965.

Grunwald, Henry, ed. *Sex in America.* New York: Bantam Books, 1964.

Hefner, Hugh M. *The Playboy Philosophy.* Chicago: HMH Publishing Co., 1962-1965.

Heschel, Abraham. *God in Search of Man.* Philadelphia: Jewish Publication Society, 1956.

Hettlinger, Richard. *Living With Sex: The Student's Dilemma.* New York: The Seabury Press, 1966.

Horowitz, George. *The Spirit of Jewish Law.* New York: Central Book Co., 1963.

Jakobovits, Immanuel. *Jewish Medical Ethics.* New York: Bloch Publishing Co., 1959.

Jastrow, Marcus. *Dictionary of the Targumim . . . Midrashic Literature.* Vols. I-II. New York: Title Publishing Company, 1943.

Jewish Encyclopedia. 12 vols. New York: Ktav Publishing House, Inc. Reprint (no date).

Kahana, K. *The Concept of Marriage in Jewish Law.* Leiden: E. J. Brill, 1966.

Katz, Jacob. *Tradition and Crisis.* Glencoe, Ill.: Free Press, 1961.

Kirkendall, Lester. *Premarital Intercourse and Interpersonal Relationships.* New York: Julian Press, 1961.

Lorenz, Konrad. *On Aggression.* New York: Harcourt, Brace and World, Inc., 1966.

Mace, David. *Hebrew Marriage.* London: Epworth Press, 1953.

Mailer, Norman. *An American Dream.* New York: Dial Press, 1965.

Maimonides, Moses. *The Guide of the Perplexed.* Translated by Shlomo Pines. Chicago: University of Chicago Press, 1963.

Marcuse, Herbert. *Eros and Civilization.* Boston: Beacon Press, 1955.

Moore, George Foot. *Judaism.* Cambridge, Mass.: Harvard University Press, 1932.

Neuman, Abraham. *The Jews in Spain.* Vols. I-II. Philadelphia: Jewish Publication Society, 1944.

Patai, Raphael. *Sex and Family in the Bible and the Middle East.* Garden City, N.Y.: Doubleday, 1959.

Philo. *The Special Laws.* Loeb Classical Library. Cambridge, Mass.: Harvard University Press.

Reich, Wilhelm. *The Function of the Orgasm.* New York: Orgone Institute Press, 1948.

Reiss, Ira. *Premarital Sexual Standards in America.* Glencoe, Ill.: Free Press, 1960.

Rhymes, Douglas. *No New Morality.* Indianapolis, Ind.: Bobbs-Merrill, 1964.

Robinson, John A. T. *Christian Morals Today.* Philadelphia: Westminster Press, 1964.

Robinson, John A. T. *Honest To God*. Philadelphia: Westminster Press, 1963.

Roth, Cecil. *The History of the Jews of Italy*. Philadelphia: Jewish Publication Society, 1946.

Roth, Cecil. *The Jews in the Renaissance*. Philadelphia: Jewish Publication Society, 1959.

Schauss, Hayyim. *The Lifetime of a Jew*. Cincinnati: Union of American Hebrew Congregations, 1950.

Schechter, Solomon. *Aspects of Rabbinic Theology*. New York: Schocken Books, 1961.

Scholem, Gershom G. *Major Trends in Jewish Mysticism*. New York: Schocken Books, 1946.

Steiman, Sidney. *Custom and Survival*. New York: Bloch Publishing Company, 1963.

Stolper, Pinchas. *The Road to Responsible Jewish Adulthood*. New York: Union of Orthodox Jewish Congregations of America, Youth Division, 1967.

von Rad, Gerhard. *Old Testament Theology*. 2 vols. New York: Harper and Row, 1962 and 1966.

Waite, A. E. *The Holy Kabbalah*. New Hyde Park, N.Y.: University Books, 1960.

Wisdom, John. *Logic and Sexual Morality*. Baltimore: Penguin, 1965.

Wolf, Arnold J., ed. *Rediscovering Judaism*. Chicago: Quadrangle Books, 1965.

Zborowski and Herzog. *Life Is With People*. New York: Schocken Books, 1962.

Zimmels, H. J. *Ashkenazim and Sephardim*. London: Oxford University Press, 1958.

ARTICLES

Bamberger, Bernard. "Qetanah, Na'arah, Bogereth," *Hebrew Union College Annual*, Vol. XXXII (Cincinnati, 1961).

Cox, Harvey. "Evangelical Ethics and the Ideal of Chastity," *Christianity and Crisis*, Vol. XXIV, No. 7, April 27, 1964.

Epstein, Louis. "The Institution of Concubinage Among the Jews," *Proceedings of the American Academy of Jewish Research*, Vol. 6, 1934-35.

Journal of Social Issues, Vol. XXII, No. 2, entitled "The Sexual Renaissance in America," April 1966.

Niebuhr, Reinhold. "Christian Attitudes Toward Sex and Family," *Christianity and Crisis,* Vol. XXIV, No. 7, April 27, 1964.

Ramsey, Paul. "A Christian Approach to Sexual Relations," *The Journal of Religion,* Vol. XLV, 1965.

Springer, Robert H., S.J. "Notes on Moral Theology: July-December, 1966," *Theological Studies,* Vol. 28, No. 2, June 1967.

BOOKS IN HEBREW

Asher ben Yehiel. *She. Utesh. Harosh.* New York: Grossman, 1954.

Chavel, Hayim David. *Kitvei Rabenu Mosheh ben Nahman.* Vol. 1. Jerusalem: Mosad Harav Kuk, 1963.

Danziger, Anshel. *Sefer Likutei Tzevi.* Sulzbach: Seckel ben Aharon, 1797.

Emden, Jacob. *Sheelat Yavetz.* Parts 1-2. New York: Gross, 1944.

Entziklopedyah Mikrait. Vol. 2. Jerusalem: Mosad Bialik, 1954.

Entziklopedyah Talmudit. Vols. 1-12. Jerusalem, 1955-67.

Falk, Zeev W. *Halakhah Umaaseh Bemedinat Yisrael.* Jerusalem: Wahrmann, 1967.

Freiman, Abraham. *Sefer Kidushin Venisuin.* Jerusalem: Mosad Harav Kuk, 1945.

Gerondi, Nissim ben Reuben. *She. Utesh. Haran.* Sadilokov, 1944.

Gross, Mosheh David. *Otzar Haagadah.* Vol. 2. Jerusalem: Mosad Harav Kuk, 1961.

Heinemann, Isaac. *Taamei Hamitzvot.* Vol. 1. The Jewish Agency, 1959.

Isaac ben Sheshet Barfat. *She. Utesh. Bar Sheshet.* New York: Mefitzei Torah, 1954.

Katz, Jacob. *Masoret Umishbar.* Jerusalem: Mosad Bialik, 1958.

Katzenellenbogen, Meir. *She. Utesh. Mahari Mintz Umaharam Padva.* Krakau-Fischer and Deutscher, 1882.

Menahem ben Aharon ben Zerah. *Tzeidah Laderekh.* Warsaw, 1880.

Mosheh ben Maimon. *Sefer Hamitzvot Leharambam.* New York: Shurkin, 1955.

Solomon ben Adret. *She. Utesh. Rashba.* Vols. 1-7. Benei Berak 1958-Jerusalem 1960.

Tishby, Isaiah. *Mishnat Hazohar.* Vol. 2. Jerusalem: Mosad Bialik, 1961.

ARTICLES IN HEBREW

Asaf, Samuel. "Lehayei Hamishpahah shel Yehudei Bitzantz," *Jubilee Volume for Professor Krauss*, Jerusalem, 1937.

Katz, Jacob. "Nisuin Vehayei Ishut Bemotzaei Yemei Habeinayim," *Tziyon*, Tenth Year.